Card-Based Control Systems for a Lean Work Design

The Fundamentals of Kanban, ConWIP, POLCA, and COBACABANA

T0372004

Card-Based Control Systems for a Lean Work Design

The Fundamentals of Kanban, ConWIP, POLCA, and COBACABANA

Matthias Thürer
Mark Stevenson
Charles Protzman

CRC Press
Taylor & Francis Group
Boca Raton   London   New York

CRC Press is an imprint of the
Taylor & Francis Group, an **informa** business

A PRODUCTIVITY PRESS BOOK

CRC Press
Taylor & Francis Group
6000 Broken Sound Parkway NW, Suite 300
Boca Raton, FL 33487-2742

Printed on acid-free paper
Version Date: 20160113

International Standard Book Number-13: 978-1-4987-4694-6 (Paperback)

Library of Congress Cataloging-in-Publication Data

Names: Thurer, Matthias author. | Stevenson, Mark (Industrial engineer),
author. | Protzman, Charles, author.
Title: Card-based control systems for a lean work design : the fundamentals
of kanban, ConWIP, POLCA, and COPACABANA / authors, Matthias Thurer, Mark
Stevenson, Charles Protzman.
Description: Boca Raton : Taylor & Francis, 2016. | Includes bibliographical
references and index.
Identifiers: LCCN 2015047911 | ISBN 9781498746946 (pbk. : alk. paper)
Subjects: LCSH: Production control. | Inventory control. | Lean
manufacturing. | Card system in business.
Classification: LCC TS155.8 .T485 2016 | DDC 658.5--dc23
LC record available at http://lccn.loc.gov/2015047911

Visit the Taylor & Francis Web site at
http://www.taylorandfrancis.com

and the CRC Press Web site at
http://www.crcpress.com

Contents

List of Figures

List of Tables

Preface

The coordination of product and/or service flows through a set of capacity resources that transform inputs, including materials, people, and information, into final products/services is one of the most challenging tasks in operations management. In recent decades, many shops have simplified this task by using card-based systems, such as *kanban*, constant work-in-process (ConWIP), and paired-cell overlapping loops of cards with authorization (POLCA). These systems provide a simple, visual approach to controlling product and/or service flows and have helped many shops reduce costly buffers while maintaining short lead times. However, there are still many shops that have not implemented such a system; and there are shops where an implementation either has failed or has not lived up to the hype. We argue that this is due to a poor fit between the characteristics of the shop's control problem and the control solution being applied.

The approach typically adopted in the academic literature is to present a particular panacea—most notably *kanban*—and then to argue that the product/service control problem (hereafter referred to as "the control problem") should be adapted to fit the solution. In other words, a solution is presented before the control problem is determined. Since there are several solutions to choose from, managers are forced to make their choice and then try to adapt their control problem accordingly so it can be handled by the solution. This appears to run counter to reason, which would argue that the nature of the problem should first be diagnosed before the solution is devised. While some adaptation of the control problem and/or solution may still be necessary, this will be a much better starting point.

Consequently, our book is different from the typical approach—as it starts with an introduction to the control *problem*, not the control *solution*. We outline how the problems encountered in typical manufacturing shops and service providers can be characterized, which allows for problem diagnosis.

We then discuss four alternative card-based control solutions, each developed to address a specific type of control problem. Exactly how each card-based control system works then emerges out of this discussion.

The first four chapters of our book (Chapters 1 through 4) lay the groundwork for problem diagnosis. We start by explaining how we conceptualize a production/service system. Here, we also locate the function of a card-based control system—i.e. what, in general, it can and cannot do. Next, we explore the underlying principle shared by all card-based control systems discussed here—input/output control, whereby the input of work is aligned with the output rate of the shop. Input/output control stabilizes the workload in the system, but it does not control the priority of orders (and thus their progress) on the shop floor. This priority is determined by a dispatching rule, as will be discussed in Chapter 3. Chapter 4 then discusses our four criteria for control problem diagnosis:

- To-stock or to-order, i.e. whether or not demand precedes production;
- The customer penetration point (or inventory/order separation point), i.e. where in the production/service process it is that material is assigned to a customer and the "order" is created;
- Routing variability, i.e. variability in the sequence and number of stations that have to be visited to produce the output; and
- Processing time variability, i.e. the degree of variability in the amount of time it takes to complete each operation in the production/service process.

The next three chapters of our book (Chapters 5 through 7) then discuss, in sequence, each of our three "traditional" card-based control systems: *kanban*, ConWIP, and POLCA. In addition to these "traditional" card-based control systems, this is the first book that discusses

1. COBACABANA (control of balance by card-based navigation), a system developed for high-variety shops producing made-to-order, customized products (in Chapter 8); and
2. How due dates or delivery time allowances can be estimated through the use of cards (in Chapter 9). This extends the scope of card-based systems, which are usually restricted to controlling work on the shop floor. This makes card-based control a complete solution as it eliminates the need for software solutions to support higher-level planning, such as tendering (or bidding) and order acceptance.

Each of the four card-based systems (*kanban*, ConWIP, POLCA, and COBACABANA) was developed for a certain need. This means that each has certain characteristics that determine its applicability. During our discussion of how each system functions, we will see how it measures up against the criteria put forward for problem diagnosis. We assess why a solution applies to a certain control problem and discuss why it should not be applied to other problems. So our focus is not only on what each system can do but also on what each cannot do.

While we discuss each system individually, it is also important to stress that the systems can be combined, where necessary—in a nested control solution. This is addressed in our final chapter, Chapter 10. This chapter also contrasts the different card-based systems, providing an overview of the

- Differences in the structure of each card-based system, i.e. from where information "flows," and where it goes;
- The different meanings of cards, i.e. what information flows; and
- The degree of support required from information technology (IT).

We contrast these characteristics with the characteristics of the typical control problems; and we discuss what this means for the application of the different card-based control systems in practice. This will help you choose the most appropriate solution for your shop. A short summary of each system—as a fast lookup—is also provided in the appendix. The overall structure of the book is summarized in Figure 0.1.

Our book seeks to bridge the practice–research divide. It emerged out of a lively discussion between the industry and academic worlds, which are represented by the authors of the book: Mark and Matthias on the academic/research side and Charles with invaluable practical experience. While it is mainly addressed to and written for practitioners, it is not a typical "management book"—rather it is a research book on the fundamentals of card-based systems written for managers. We therefore hope that it will also be of value to researchers, students, and anyone interested in the challenging world of operations management.

Finally, before starting the book, it is important to acknowledge *what we don't do*. First, we do not focus on highlighting the results of previous studies on card-based systems, because these results will only be achieved if the right system is chosen for the control problem—there is no point being persuaded by performance results that might not be achievable. Second, we also do not focus on outlining a detailed implementation blueprint, because there

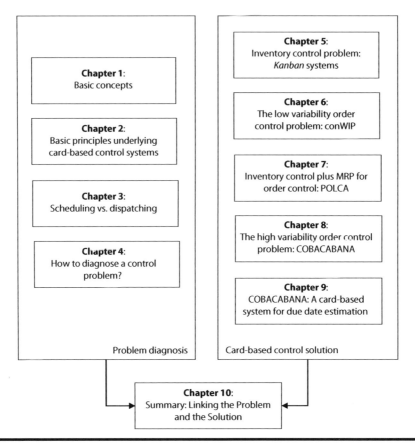

Figure 0.1   Structure of the book.

is no single formula that works for every organization—they are all different. Instead, we hope that this book will provide you with a guide for a problem diagnosis that helps move toward finding the right solution to your particular control problem. But the solutions presented here should not be considered "cookie-cutter" solutions. Yes, they provide the building blocks, but we cannot emphasize strongly enough the importance of developing a habit of continually watching your processes to discover your own solutions. We close out this preface with the following thought from Taiichi Ohno (1988, pp. 77–78), one of the pioneers of the Toyota Production System:

> With any problem I ask *why* five times. This Toyota procedure is actually adapted from Toyoda Sakichi's habit of watching. We can talk about work improvement, but unless we know production thoroughly we can accomplish nothing. Stand on the production floor all day and watch—you will eventually discover what has to be done. I cannot emphasize this too much.

Acknowledgments

We would like to acknowledge the people who have accompanied us on our quest for simple yet effective control for complex shops. While we wrote this book and are solely responsible for what it contains, most of the ideas emerged during collaboration and "endless" discussions on the subject with others. This includes (in no particular order) Martin J. Land, Lawrence D. Fredendall, Cristovao Silva, Linda Hendry, Steven A. Melnyk, George Q. Huang, Tim Qu, Hermann Lödding, Moacir Godinho Filho, Ivan Tomašević, Thomas Maschek, Shuo-Yan Chou, Pedro J. M. Martins, and Joana B. V. Marques—to name just a few.

Authors

 **Matthias Thürer** is a professor at Jinan University (People's Republic of China). He holds a master's degree from the Technical University Berlin (Germany) and a PhD from the University of Coimbra (Portugal). He maintains a broad research network, regularly visiting universities such as Lancaster University (UK), the University of Clemson (US), Michigan State University (US), and the University of Groningen (the Netherlands). Before getting involved in academia, Matthias worked in several companies, did an apprenticeship and became a master craftsman ("Meister"). Simple control for complex shops is one of Matthias's main research interests. He has published widely on production control systems and is a leading expert on workload control and COBACABANA.

 **Mark Stevenson** is a professor of operations management at Lancaster University, United Kingdom. He has a bachelor's degree and PhD from the Department of Management Science at Lancaster University Management School. Mark's PhD was on workload control, the production planning and control concept for low-volume, high-variety shops that underpins COBACABANA. Mark's research has included implementing the workload control concept in practice to learn from the implementation process and results. He has published widely in peer-reviewed academic operations management journals, including on production planning and control.

 **Charles Protzman** is an internationally renowned Lean implementer, trainer, speaker, and Shingo Prize-winning author with over 33 years' experience in materials and operations management. He has consulted with manufacturers, hospitals, government agencies, and other service industries. He has published the Shingo Prize-winning book series *Leveraging Lean in Healthcare* and plans to have an additional two books, including the *Lean Practitioner's Field Book*, published by the end of the year.

In November 1997, Charles Protzman formed Business Improvement Group (B.I.G.) LLC. B.I.G. is located in Baltimore, Maryland, and specializes in training and implementing Lean thinking principles and the Lean business delivery system—LBDS. Charles has spent the last 25 years implementing successful Lean product line conversions, kaizen events, and administrative business system improvements (transactional Lean) across the United States and internationally.

He spent 13 and a half years with AlliedSignal, now Honeywell, where he was an aerospace strategic operations manager and the first AlliedSignal Lean master. He has received numerous special recognition and cost reduction awards. Charles has taught students from all over the world in Lean principles and total quality.

He is a master facilitator and trainer in total companywide quality management, facilitation, running highly effective meetings, career development, change management, benchmarking, leadership, systems thinking, high-performance work teams, team building, Myers-Briggs Type Indicator™, Lean thinking, and supply chain management. He has also taken Baldridge Examiner training and Six Sigma Black Belt management courses.

Charles has a BA and an MBA from Loyola University in Maryland. He is currently a member of SME, Association for Manufacturing Excellence (AME), Institute of Industrial Engineers (IIE), American Society for Quality (ASQ), and the Association for Psychological Type. He is a charter certified Myers-Briggs Type Indicator™ (MBTI) instructor (#C10083). He was a past member of the American Production and Inventory Control Society (APICS), AME Champions Club, and National Association of Purchasing Management (NAPM).

Chapter 1

Basic Concepts

Highlights

- *We outline how we conceptualize a production/service system and the business operations/processes executed.*
- *We outline what a card-based control system does.*
- *We outline what a card-based control system does not do.*
- *We make some important points concerning why you should choose a card-based control system rather than the latest technology.*

This book promises to be different. Earlier books have typically focused on one particular card-based control system before presenting environments where it is argued that they provide the best solution. This creates the approach of putting the solution ahead of determining the problem.

In contrast, we first discuss how to diagnose a problem and then discuss a range of possible solutions from which to choose. This seems more logical, but it is a much more complicated task, since we cannot start directly by presenting a well-defined solution. Rather, we first have to build the foundations for diagnosing the problem that your shop is faced with; and we must do this for a problem that we all know is quite complex:

> *The coordination of product/service flows through a set of capacity resources, in your shop, that transform materials, people, information, etc., into final products/services.*

From here on in, we call this "the control problem." This control problem is complex since resources are typically scarce and/or constrained; and because different product/service flows often compete for the same resources.

Before starting any diagnosis, we must take a step back and introduce some basic concepts. We first need to understand how a production/service system can be described. This then clarifies the role that card-based control systems can and cannot play in supporting such a system. It is also important that we use the same concepts throughout the book to provide the required clarity. You may find this somewhat technical, but bear with us. We will use a lot of *"timeouts"* to give you some breathing space, some time to conceptualize things and perhaps to relate them to your own shop.

You may agree or disagree with our conceptual definitions. That is fine. There is no "true" conceptualization of a production/service system. But what is important is that you understand how we define and use the concepts in this book. Only this will make our suggestions on how to diagnose a control problem (and consequently use the most suitable control solution) clear. But let's just start.

What Is a Production/Service System?

We start by looking at the different parts that constitute a production/ service system. We will first approach this from the perspective of the product/service. Thus, we describe a production/service system in terms of its product/service flows. In doing so, it is common practice to start with the input to a product/service flow. But we arbitrarily turn this around and start with the most important aspect—the customer. So let's define the first five concepts that will be used in this book to describe a product/service flow.

The Customer

One of the primary objectives of any company is to make money. Environmental and social responsibility is also important, but firms also do not need to be ashamed of the desire to be profitable. To make money—someone has to be willing to pay for something. The "someone" is the customer. The "something" is the product/service. Even though we say someone is willing to pay, sometimes no real payment takes place; for instance, if we refer to an internal customer belonging to the same company, department, operation, etc.

The Product/Service

The output is the product/service or range of products/services that you sell. If you don't sell the product, it has to be scrapped; if you don't sell the service, you waste your time (and time is money). A product needs to be produced and a service needs to be provided. So some transforming action has to take place. We call this transforming action—work.

Processes

Most work is complex enough that it is subdivided into various tasks that are performed at different stages. We consider this series of interlinked tasks or *operations* a process to accomplish work (or complete a transformation). A process is defined, for example, by the American Heritage College Dictionary as "a series of actions, changes or functions bringing about a result." The result in our case is the product/service. It is only the transforming action that is called work—any other actions (or not doing any actions) can be considered operational wastes.

Input (Supply)

Each process needs an input—something to be transformed. We call this the supply. This may be steel, patients, pizza dough, or even the sheets of paper on which this book is printed. The input, which we denote as supply, must always precede the process.

Supplier

We consider the supplier to be whoever provides the input (supply) to the process, whether it is a physical product, information, or even a customer wanting a haircut. Just like the customer, the supplier may be internal to the company, department, operation, and so on.

These five concepts can be used to describe any production/service flow. And they can be identified in practice through the use of a simple supplier of inputs for processes producing output for customers (SIPOC) analysis. SIPOC analysis is very simple—you just ask yourself who *supplies* which *input* for what *processes* that produce what *output* for which *customers*? This is why it is called SIPOC. An example of a SIPOC analysis is given in Table 1.1.

The five concepts—suppliers, supply (input), processes, product/service (output), and customer—relate to different stages or locations in the flow of products/services. In fact, each of our suppliers and customers is likely to have their own set of processes, and we could therefore create another SIPOC for each of them. In other words, SIPOC can be applied at various macro and micro levels. This could also involve identifying our suppliers' suppliers and the customers of our customers (if they are not the end-customer). Similarly, we could conduct a SIPOC for each operation of our process. The viewpoint we choose to adopt is referred to as the level of analysis.

Level of Analysis

Each organization has a vertical structure—it is likely to be part of a supply chain with other organizations; it may also have its own internal supply chain between departments, where each department has different work stations; and so on. At each of these levels, there is a flow of products/services. The vertical level at which a problem is diagnosed is called the level of analysis.

Table 1.1   Example of a SIPOC Analysis: Pizza

Pizza-Making Process A				
Supplier	*Inputs*	*Process*	*Outputs*	*Customer*
Storage	Raw materials	Create delicious pizza	Finished pizzas	You
	Input Metrics/ Specifications	*Resources*	*Output Metrics/ Specifications*	
	Product mix:	Make dough	Product mix:	
	Product types	Put cheese	Product types	
	Amounts	Inspect	Amounts	
	Sequence	Cook pizza	Sequence	
	Supply lead time	...	Supply lead time	
	Location of supply		Location of supply	
	Packaging		Packaging	
	...		...	

According to the level of analysis that we take when examining product/ service flows, we will typically talk about supply chain management, operations management, or job design.

Supply Chain Management

Links different product/service flows. These flows may be internal (within one organization) or external (between different organizations). So we can think of there as being an internal and an external supply chain.

Operations Management

This is typically internally focused, and manages the flow of independent product/service flows through a set of transforming resources.

Job Design

Focuses on the processes within a single operation.

This book is targeted at operations management, with our main focus being on the "shop." The shop can be described as the place where work is accomplished. This is the physical location where processes are realized. This may be a machine shop, a hospital, a restaurant, a hotel, a bank, a call center, etc.

Timeout: Card-based systems were mainly developed for use in manufacturing environments. One reason for their limited development in other settings is that the need for extending the benefits of best practices to other non-manufacturing operations, such as to health-care operations or even the back-office processes of manufacturing companies, has only recently been recognized. We hope that you will therefore understand if we have a certain bias toward manufacturing throughout the book. This is just a bias; it says nothing about applicability. For example, if we talk about assembly in the context of Toyota and car production, this could also be translated to the context of a patient requiring different services in a hospital.

The concept of a shop provides a different perspective to the control problem. In the previous section, we focused on the product/service flow. Operation management manages the flow of independent product/service flows through the same transforming resources. These resources (through

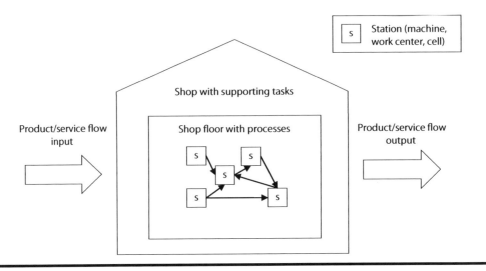

Figure 1.1 Product/service flow through the physical locations where the processes are realized.

which the product/service flow "flows") are typically located somewhere. So let's introduce some important concepts to describe where work is executed, that is, where the flow of products/services actually occurs. All three are illustrated in Figure 1.1. But first a short timeout on our metaphorical use of the term flow.

Timeout: It is clear that products typically do not flow through resources. Of course, in the chemical industry or when producing soft-drinks, they in fact do. But typically products are discrete entities and thus move from resource to resource. At each transforming resource, some transformation takes place. However, we consider the image of products flowing through different resources a powerful means to visualize a production/service system. In fact, some of the laws in operations management are directly derived from fluid mechanics.

The Shop

This is the physical location where operations and supporting tasks take place. Shops present a physical constraint on the product/service flow. Companies typically create shops according to customer demand, that is, shops serve a specific customer group. For example, your company may have a shop in different cities, or there may be two shops at the same place but with each shop producing output for different customers or market segments.

The Shop Floor

This is the physical place where operations take place. It is part of the shop (see previous definition of the Shop). The shop floor may produce different products or provide different services. These products/services may require very different processes and routings (i.e. the sequence in which stations, as defined next, must be visited).

A Station

This is the physical entity or location where an operation is executed. A shop floor typically consists of several stations. How the stations are arranged on the shop floor is referred to as the "layout."

Timeout: We define an operation from the perspective of the product/ service—a production process is what the input (product, person, etc.) experiences. This is a series of operations. A station is where the operation(s) occur.

While we commonly use the term "station" in this book, this could also be known as a work center, cell, hospital room, and so on. It is just a question of the level (or unit) of analysis and the characteristics of the product/service processes that have to be completed. It is like the definition of an operation. An operation may be a single process step, two steps, or even 100 steps. There is no clear-cut definition.

But it is very important to separate operations from stations—card-based control systems coordinate operations (and thus product/service processes) across stations. They are bound by stations since cards always circulate between stations. This sounds complex, but we think it will become clear when we discuss card-based systems in more depth later in the book.

So far, we have looked at the production/service system from two perspectives: the flow of products/services and the physical location where work is executed. The physical location poses a constraint on which resources are available. From the product/service flow perspective, SIPOC identifies the customer requirements on the system, that is, everything that takes place in between the supplier and customer (independent of whether these are viewed as being internal or external to the organization). The requirements on the system are, consequently, (i) what supply is needed;

(ii) what processes have to be accommodated; and (iii) what product/service characteristics (e.g. in terms of quality) have to be met. If different (groups of) products are produced on the same shop floor, a SIPOC should be created for each product/product group.

Next, we will take a third perspective and look at how to describe the actual transformation process, that is, the business operations.

Timeout: The difference between the three perspectives can also be illustrated by way of an example in the context of a restaurant. A restaurant has a kitchen through which food flows and is transformed from ingredients into delicious dishes (the customer orders). Suppliers provide the input (vegetables, meat, etc.) to meet requests; and these inputs are transformed through a process that converts the input into output (a delicious dish) for the customer. The SIPOC analysis gives us the receipt for each dish. Identifying the location where the cooking process will take place (in this case, the kitchen) tells us what capacity resources (stove, chefs, etc.) we can use and what physical constraints exist on the flow of materials. Next, we will look at how the actual cooking process occurs. People often tend to start with the cooking process, but the quantity of bad food that we (the writers) have produced has taught us the lesson that it is very important to look at the receipt and the kitchen first! This is why we have started the book with these two perspectives.

What Is a Business Operation/Process?

To adequately describe a business process, we first have to describe a business operation. Three variables are required for a business operation to occur (see Figure 1.2):

1. Transforming resources, that is, the capacity of facilities, your shop's equipment (e.g. computer numerically controlled (CNC) and numerically controlled (NC) machines, computed tomography (CT) and magnetic resonance imaging (MRI) scanners, copiers, pizza ovens, etc.), and human resources (operators/staff/doctors/nurses, etc.).
2. Transformed resources, i.e. material, people, or information inflows that have been and/or are waiting to be transformed.
3. Resource requirements, i.e. customer demand (quantities, specifications, etc.) for products requiring transforming and transformed resources.

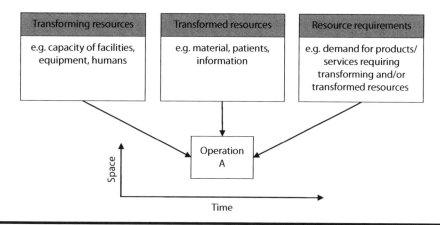

Figure 1.2 Three variables—transforming resources, transformed resources, and resource requirements—are required for an operation to occur.

Transforming Resources (Capacity)

Transforming resources are resources that realize the actions, changes, or functions that bring about the results. This may be machines or humans (or living beings in general).

Timeout: We have introduced a distinction between the shop/shop floor/station as the location where the operation is executed and the actual transforming resources. This distinction is often blurred in the book since all card-based systems assume transforming resources (machines or humans) await the stream of transformed resources (e.g. products or patients) at the location. But it is acknowledged that this assumption might not always apply, such as when building big products (like shipbuilding), or when transforming resources also have to be coordinated. An example for the latter is an operating room (station) where we have to control the flow of transformed resources (the patients) and transforming resources (the surgeons). This is normally done by first scheduling the surgeons and then coordinating the flow of patients through the shop.

Transformed Resources (Inventory and Work-in-Process)

Transformed resources are the materials, people (e.g. patients), information, etc. that receive the action—i.e. are to be transformed. In this book, we will distinguish between three types of transformed resources:

1. The transformed resources that precede the process—these are considered supply.

2. The transformed resources in the process—these are considered work-in-process (WIP) inventory.
3. The transformed resources after completion of the whole process—these are considered finished goods inventory.

Resource Requirements (Customer Demand)

The customer is willing to pay for work. This work is a set of operations. An operation requires a certain set of transformed and transforming resources. Therefore, we denote customer demand as resource requirements.

If any of these three variables is missing, a business operation cannot occur. Rather, some form of waste is created, e.g. in the form of inventory waste (when transformed resources wait for transforming resources and/ or resource requirements), waiting waste (when transforming resources wait for transformed resources and/or resource requirements), or overproduction (when transformed resources wait for resource requirements).

Therefore, transformed resources, transforming resources, and resource requirements have to be synchronized in terms of time, space, and quality. The business process (i.e. a set of business operations) will be most effective and efficient if coordination is perfect—i.e. the right operation (in terms of customer demand) occurs at the right time at the right place—but this rarely, if ever, happens. Rather, some form of "waste" occurs. The coordination in terms of time and space is the job of the *production control system* (whether this is card based or otherwise). Quality control's job is to make sure the variables are of the right quality.

A Card-Based Control System

A production control system that coordinates a set of business operations (i.e. business processes) to synchronize transforming resources, transformed resources, and resource requirements. In this book, when we talk about card-based systems, we will be referring to the following control systems: *kanban*, constant work-in-process (ConWIP), paired-cell overlapping loops of cards with authorization (POLCA), and control of balance by card-based navigation (COBACABANA) (to be defined properly later in the book). All four of these control systems include control of the input of work to the shop floor in accordance with the output of work from the shop floor. Feedback on the output from a station or the shop floor is typically provided by cards (or some other physical means of communicating or signaling information). This is why they are called card-based systems.

What Does a Card-Based Control System Actually Control?

One of the main objectives of management should be waste reduction, since reducing waste is an enabler for increasing profitability and market share.

This is the sort of statement that you have probably heard many times before. But ask others how waste is defined, and you will rarely get the same answer twice. In fact, we suspect that inconsistencies between what different people mean when they talk about waste has led many people to abandon the waste concept altogether. On the contrary, we believe "waste" is an extremely powerful concept when properly understood and applied. More importantly for this book, it highlights how a card-based control system can contribute to improved performance. So let's start with a definition of the waste concept.

Waste

There is no "positive" definition of waste, i.e. what it is. Rather, waste is defined "negatively" by what it is not. It can be defined by two aspects:

1. Waste is any system input (in terms of transforming and transformed resources) that is *not* transformed into an output (fulfilled customer demand or what the customer is willing to pay for), i.e. waste = system input – system output.
2. Waste is any output or transformation that does *not* occur just-in-time, i.e. waste occurs when the transformation is not synchronized with the timing of customer demand. A transformation too early will result in overproduction; and overproduction results in increased inventory, transportation, etc. A transformation too late will result in unfulfilled customer demand.

Timeout: The focus of card-based control systems, and thus of this book, is on the second aspect of waste. According to Taiichi Ohno (1988), just-in-time is one of the two pillars of the Toyota Production System.

Just-in-time essentially means that transforming resources, transformed resources, and resource requirements are available/used at the right time, in the right place, and in the right quantity. While the need for not delivering "too late" has always been recognized (since an angry customer makes it often quite clear), the need for not producing too early is a seminal contribution from Taiichi Ohno's work. In fact, one of his main worries was that his workers produced too much—i.e. overproduction. The kanban *system was developed to curb overproduction. Overproduction may not have been a problem in a mass production environment—as everything that could be produced would probably be sold eventually. But with the advent of global competition and customization, these times and shops have largely disappeared.*

The other pillar is autonomation, or automation with a human touch; according to Monden (1983), autonomation mainly relates to autonomous defect control (p. 2)—it is the autonomous check on abnormality in a process (p. 10). So autonomation refers to ensuring transformed and transforming resources are of the right quality.

Categories of Waste

According to its position in the system, Ohno (1988) categorized waste into seven categories (see Table 1.2). These categories were split by Shigeo Shingo (1989), into two dimensions, depending on whether we focus on the flow of transformed resources through the shop floor—the *product/service flow*—or on the *operations*, which are the actions taken to accomplish the transformation. The former is called *process waste* and the latter is called *operational waste*.

Timeout: Card-based control systems directly impact inventory, waiting, and overproduction wastes. Waiting is affected in two ways—it is reduced, and it is postponed. If a shop is not running at 100% utilization (which seems likely), the transforming resource will be waiting (i.e. starving or idle) for a certain proportion of time (100% minus the utilization level). It is important that the transforming resource does not wait when there is suitable work ready to be processed. However, waiting waste, if there is no work, is preferable to overproduction. This was a major point highlighted by Taiichi Ohno. The difference between waiting and inventory waste only becomes clear when taking two different perspectives. A waiting transformed resource (i.e. the product/service flow) is called inventory waste. A waiting transforming resource is called waiting waste. We discussed these two dimensions in

Table 1.2   The Seven Wastes

The Seven Wastes	Definition	Example (Making a Cheese Sandwich)
Waiting	Part of operations. Any delay in the actions that accomplish process transformations.	You are ready to fill the sandwich, but your wife comes and blocks the fridge so you have to wait.
Overproduction	Part of operations. Anticipated process transformations; producing too much.	While your wife blocks the fridge you just start on another sandwich for tomorrow.
Unnecessary motion	Part of operations. Any action that does not transform the product/service, adding value.	You prepare the whole sandwich (without cheese) and then open it once more to put the cheese in.
Overprocessing	Part of the product/service flow. Producing anything which is not valued by the customer. Value engineering and value analysis must be carried out first. Instead of focusing merely on efficiency, the question is why we make a given product/service and use a given method.	You melt the cheese but your wife didn't ask for melted cheese on her sandwich.
Transportation	Part of the product/service flow. Any movement of material or products.	You take the cheese sandwich with you from the work surface/counter to the fridge, then set it on the counter while you get your cheese. Then you move it back to the counter.
Inventory	Part of the product/service flow. Work-in-process (and related process delays); finished goods inventory.	You have several sandwiches waiting for cheese, some waiting to be wrapped, and some wrapped waiting for the bag.
Defects	Part of the product/service flow. Any quality loss, expressed as rework or scrap.	Oh no, you forgot the cheese!

Source: Based on Ohno, T. *Toyota Production System: Beyond Large-Scale Production,* 1st edn., Productivity Press, Cambridge, MA, 1988; Shingo, S., *A Study of the Toyota Production System from an Industrial Engineering Viewpoint,* Productivity Press, Cambridge, MA, 1989.

this chapter when defining production control as being the coordination of product/service processes through a set of capacity resources.

A system without any waste is an ideal system in which transformed resources, transforming resources, and resource requirements meet at the right time, in the right place, in the right quantity, and at the right level of quality. But such a system is unlikely to exist in reality—if there is variability/uncertainty (in supply, demand, quality, etc.) then there will always be some form of waste. And some level of variability/uncertainty is inevitable. Therefore, we will further define two waste types based on their dependence on variability/uncertainty.

Types of Waste

We can define two types of waste:

- Obvious waste (Type I waste): Any waste that can be reduced without creating another form of waste.
- Buffer waste (Type II waste): Any waste that cannot be reduced without creating another form of waste.

An example of an obvious waste (Type I) is the needless, repetitive movement of personnel due to poor shop layout or job design. Meanwhile, buffer waste (Type II) draws on Hopp and Spearman's (2004, p. 145) argument that, when variability exists, it will be buffered somehow. Reducing a waste that is due to variability/uncertainty without reducing the source of the variability/uncertainty itself will only lead to the creation of another form of waste, perhaps at the same or another point in the system—we call this waste migration.

Waste Migration

If buffer waste is reduced without variability/uncertainty reduction, it will migrate, i.e. it will appear at another point in the system or another form of waste may be created by the system.

Timeout: The difference between the two waste types is very important in practice. For example, Taiichi Ohno stated that only a company with perfect coordination of transformed resources, transforming resources, and resource requirements should approach zero inventory. All other companies will just create another waste category; so they would be "zero inventory" but not "zero waste."

Waste migration makes inventory reduction a moving target; and it may explain the failure of many companies that have tried to implement zero inventory to obtain improved coordination. Card-based control systems affect both types of waste: obvious waste and buffer waste. However, reducing buffer waste requires some form of variability reduction. How this is realized (e.g. through feedback loops on the workload situation on the shop floor, starvation avoidance, or load balancing) will be discussed in Chapters 5 through 9 when we discuss the different card-based control systems.

You may have wondered why we write variability/uncertainty and not just variability. We will differentiate between variability and uncertainty in this book as follows:

Variability

Variability is any deviation from the average.

Uncertainty

Uncertainty is the probability or risk of something unexpected happening.

For example, when Carnival or Easter takes place is highly variable but far from uncertain. Variability is a property of a set of measured values or data (and so is independent from the real world). Uncertainty says something about how valid these measures/data are (and so links the measure to the world). Buffer waste can be optimized for variability, but for uncertainty it is a question of how much risk a manager is willing to take. The same difference is often expressed as predictable and unpredictable variability. As said before, for us it is not important which word is used to express this important difference. What is important is to recognize that there is a difference.

Timeout: The amount of inventory in a system is generally proportionate to the perceived inherent risk (see e.g. Beer 1994, pp. 176–177). Both too little and too much inventory can be perceived as risk. The first bears the risk of unfulfilled customer demand. The second bears the risk, e.g. of obsolescence.

This is also referred to as the newsvendor problem in analogy to the problem of a newspaper seller who must decide how many copies of the day's newspapers to stock in the face of uncertain demand and knowing that unsold copies will be worthless at the end of the day.

Waste Reduction

This all results in a three-dimensional waste framework, as illustrated in Figure 1.3. Each waste category/type requires a different set of tools for reduction/elimination. In general, there are three interrelated approaches to waste reduction:

1. To eliminate obvious waste
2. To reduce variability and/or uncertainty, transforming buffers into obvious waste
3. To balance or swap buffers to best achieve performance targets

Timeout: Card-based control systems aim to achieve #2 through the coordination of transformed resources (materials, people, information, etc.), transforming resources (people, machines, etc.), and resource requirements (customer demand). They allow for reducing waste such as inventory, waiting, and overproduction. However, wastes such as overprocessing, quality defects, and unnecessary motions are not directly impacted by card-based

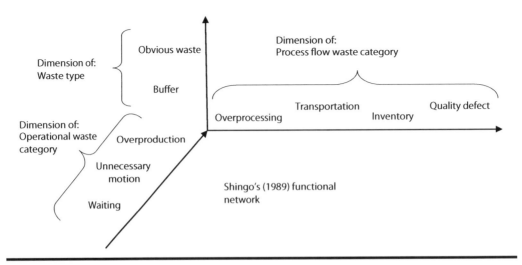

Figure 1.3   Waste dimensions—extending Shingo's (1989) two-dimensional waste network.

control systems. So they always need to be supported by additional tools and/ or initiatives (e.g. Lean/quality).

We have argued above that zero waste presupposes an ideal system. Consequently, we have to introduce another important concept that provides the target conditions for your shop and, consequently, the card-based control system—waste allowance.

Waste Allowance

This is the waste that is *allowed by the customer.* It is typically a result of negotiation. Examples are price and customer delivery time (i.e. the time when the customer expects the product/service to be available). The former allows for waste and incurred cost (customer's price = direct material + direct labor + waste), while the latter allows for waste and resulting process delays (customer delivery time – time of customer order = time allowance).

Timeout: An example of the price allowance is target costing. For example, many tools for waste reduction were developed by Toyota while attempting to build the $1,000 car (Hino 2006). But anyone that has ordered a pizza understands delivery time allowances. We will later discover that a delivery time allowance larger than (approximately) zero only occurs in a specific kind of company—companies that assemble, produce, build, and serve "to-order." Companies that produce "to-stock" (and deliver from stock) are expected by the customer to have a zero delivery time (ignoring transportation to the customer of course, which is considered to be outside of the control problem).

Meanwhile, the cost allowance leads to another important point. Our waste categories introduced in this chapter are defined operationally. But there can be important differences in terms of the financial impact. For example, a waiting (bought) machine and a waiting worker are both waiting waste. But, for the machine, you may only have the one-time acquisition cost and, after some years, the asset is depreciated. Meanwhile, workers' salaries typically increase over time, and they have to be paid each month. This is why Taiichi Ohno introduced the concept of one operator using several machines. Toyota increased machine capacity (waiting waste) to reduce human capacity. Capacity could then be adjusted easily (in terms of the number of machines handled by one worker) while maintaining the same cost (the salary of the one worker).

Waste reduction is not a means by itself but should be applied to allow for more competitive waste allowances and, consequently, provide better service to the customer.

Why Use a Card-Based Control System Rather than the Latest Technology?

You may wonder why you should invest time and effort in a card-based system. After all, we live in a digital age. There is the Internet of Things (IoT), enterprise resource planning (ERP) systems, advanced planning and scheduling (APS) systems, etc.

This prompts two questions:

1. Why should you use a card-based control system?
2. Why should you use cards?

Card-based control systems are quite simple (yet extremely effective). We will see in the next chapter that their main feature is a feedback loop, which ensures that only the products needed are produced and that only the services needed are provided. Now, using feedback on the actual situation to guide decisions rather than blindly following a production plan (even if the situation for which the plan has been developed has been dramatically changed) seems quite obvious—but did you ever ask yourself what is the logic used for controlling production/services that underpins the latest ERP software? Often this logic is not even explicit—these systems can remain a "black box" to the user, who is in the hands of the consultant that configured the software or the people updating (or generally not updating) the data in the system.

Timeout: You should always keep in mind that most planning software is designed to be sold (just create a SIPOC and see yourself as the customer). So something new must be invented all the time, even if there is already something existing that solves the problem. But ask yourself—from a company perspective—do you need a car that goes and goes and goes, or do you need a fancy car that breaks down every 1,000 kilometers? ERP systems have many bells and whistles, but the logic underpinning their material requirements planning (MRP) functionality, for example, has not changed dramatically since the approach was introduced in the 1970s. The technology has developed rapidly, but the production control theory incorporated has not developed at the same rate.

- So a first answer to question (i) is that card-based control systems make more sense since they use feedback on the actual situation to produce/ provide only what is needed.
- A second answer to (i) is that card-based control systems are simple to implement—in fact, we just have feedback loops of cards and typically no complicated calculations hidden somewhere (i.e. buried in inaccessible software coding).
- A third answer to (i) is that card-based control systems are extremely cheap and much more accurate when compared to software. Moreover, you do not need updates, patches, new versions or servers, etc. And no one can hack into your card system. In fact, a drawback of software is that you always require an update, which of course costs money and never goes smoothly. In effect, a software implementation is never really complete. This is how software firms survive. To find (or design) a card-based system that can work for you, you just have to read this book. Of course, time and effort will also be needed to implement the ideas, as is the case for any new improvement initiative or innovation.
- Also, unexpected computer shutdowns won't affect your production. Likewise, the dreaded Y2K (year 2000) problem would not have been an issue for card-based systems.

Timeout: You should always keep in mind that you invest in a control system to solve problems, not to create new ones. It makes no sense to implement a new system where you end up with more problems in terms of getting it in place and running it than it actually solves.

Let's now address question (ii). The answer is simple:

- First, cards are visual, physical entities. In fact, the basic idea of radio frequency identification devices and other sensors used as part of the IoT and Industry 4.0 is to provide feedback that is similar to cards. But they just provide bits and bytes—i.e. data.
- Second, a card always provides information. Did you ever ask yourself what happens with all the data accumulated by the latest IT solution (if its implementation is successfully achieved)? Well, just look at the latest job recruitment page—people are desperate for big data analysts to get

some information out of their data. And once you get the information, is it still the right information (i.e. is it the information you need at the time you need it)? Cards provide the necessary information, simply and visually. And they provide it when it is needed.

Timeout: That cards are physical objects may not seem important, but we argue that it is. Cards ensure information does not get lost since neither an existing nor a missing card can be ignored. If a card is lying somewhere or is missing then this is a physical fact, which calls for attention.

Of course there are also drawbacks to physical cards since they need to be moved to transmit information. Here new technology, as provided by the Internet of Things, may in fact help. But new technology should maintain the function of cards (as being visual information that is needed) and card-based control systems (as being simple). In fact, rather than being substituted by new technology, card-based control systems may inform the structure for the Internet of Things so it can be effectively used for production control.

In other words, are you sure that the extra data and information provided by your IT system is really useful and not simply overproduction waste? Or, as Taiichi Ohno already questioned in the 1980s when personal computers became popular,

> Is it really economical to provide more information than we need—more quickly than we need it? This is like buying a large, high-performance machine that produces too much. The extra items have to be stored in a warehouse, which raises the cost. Much of the excess information generated by computers is not needed for production at all. (Ohno, 1988, p. 47)

Finally, Table 1.3 summarizes why you should use a card-based control system.

Summary: What Card-Based Control Systems Do (And What They Do Not Do)

The objective of card-based control systems is the coordination of transforming resources, transformed resources, and resource requirements such that the operations of a process are realized efficiently and on time. It is a tool to

Table 1.3   Some Good Reasons Why You Should Use a Card-Based Control System

Why Should You Use a Card-Based Control System?	Why Should You Use Cards?
Uses feedback on the current situation on the shop floor. Ensures that only the products needed are used and that only the services needed are provided. Is simple in application. Uses clear and visual logic.	Cards are visual. Cards signal the information needed for production when it is needed. They avoid the overproduction of information. They are simple. They are cheap.

realize just-in-time—one of the two pillars of the Toyota Production System (the other being autonomation, or automation with a human touch). But it is not a solution to all problems! In fact, it must be supported by other Lean/quality tools if it is to be effective.

Let's start with the major misconceptions related to card-based control systems—what they do not do:

- Card-based control systems do not ensure quality. They may positively impact quality by reducing work-in-process levels—but nothing more. Ensuring quality is the job of, for example, total quality management (TQM) or Six Sigma.
- Card-based control systems do not improve the effectiveness of the process. In other words, they do not ensure that the resource requirements given to the shop actually represent what the customer wants. Often it is design and engineering or marketing that determine what is produced, i.e. the resource requirements.
- Card-based control systems do not improve the efficiency of an operation itself—i.e. reduce unnecessary motions. This is the job of motion studies, improved job design, or improved product design.
- Card-based control systems do not make your unreliable machines more reliable. This is the job of, for example, total productive maintenance (TPM).
- Card-based control systems do not reduce transportation waste or set-up times. This is the job of, for example, workplace organization methods, e.g. sort (straighten or set in order), store, shine, standardize, and sustain (5 S) and single-minute exchange of die (SMED).

Timeout: This book is about the advantages of card-based control systems. So you may be wondering why we put so much emphasis here on what these systems do not do rather than on "selling" what they actually do. This goes back to the premise of our book. It is important that you are sure that card-based control—i.e. the coordination of your business operations/processes—is the root cause of your problems. The objective of your company should be ongoing sustainable waste reduction. A card-based control system is only one (probably necessary) tool to achieve this. If your problem is quality or equipment availability, spending a lot of effort on implementing a card-based control system is, at the moment, probably not the right solution (although it may help to support other tools to address these problems).

It is also important for the premise of this book that we understand what card-based control systems do actually achieve:

- Card-based control systems reduce uncertainty in the control decision by using feedback loops that update the current situation on the shop floor in real-time.
- Card-based control systems coordinate the flow of products/services through the system. Improving the flow provides a means of reducing inventory; keep in mind that inventory waste is any delay in the flow of transformed resources. Card-based systems reduce obvious inventory waste and, through improved coordination (i.e. reduced variability), reduce buffer inventory waste.
- Card-based control systems coordinate the flow of products/services in accordance with the availability of transforming resources. This allows for the postponement of waiting waste. In most shops, waiting necessarily occurs. Only a shop with 100% utilization has no waiting; but such a shop would most probably have inventory (delayed transformed resources) or overproduction (anticipated transformation) waste.
- Card-based control systems reduce waiting waste, i.e. they free up capacity. Waiting becomes obvious waste, meaning it can be eliminated, if there are no resource requirements for which the transforming resources are waiting. In this case, transforming resources can be used for other tasks without jeopardizing the production process.
- Card-based control systems avoid overproduction, as highlighted by Taiichi Ohno—waiting should not be transformed into overproduction.

Table 1.4   What Card-Based Control Systems Do and What They Don't Do

Card-Based Control Systems Do Not	*Card-Based Control Systems Help Your Company To*
Ensure quality;	Reduce uncertainty in control
Improve effectiveness;	decisions;
Improve operational efficiencies;	Reduce inventory waste;
Make unreliable machines more reliable; or	Postpone waiting waste;
Reduce transportation waste or set-up	Reduce waiting waste; and
times	Avoid overproduction

In particular, the *kanban* system was developed specifically to curb overproduction. This is achieved by withholding work from the shop floor that is not needed.

The main points on what card-based control systems do and what they don't do are summarized in Table 1.4.

Highlights Revisited

■ *We outline how we conceptualize a production/service system and the business operations/processes executed.* Transformed resources flow through transforming resources whereby they are transformed. The transforming actions are called operations. A series of operations is a process. The outcome of the process is the product/service.

■ *We outline what a card-based control system does.* Card-based control systems aim to reduce variability and/or uncertainty through the coordination of transformed resources (materials, people, information, etc.), transforming resources (people, machines, etc.), and resource requirements (customer demand). This transforms buffers into obvious waste, which then can be eliminated. Card-based systems allow for reducing wastes such as inventory, waiting, and overproduction.

■ *We outline what a card-based control system does not do.* Card-based control systems do not directly improve quality or the efficiency of your operations. They also do not make unreliable machines more reliable or your workers more motivated.

■ *We make some important points concerning why you should choose a card-based control system rather than the latest technology.* Card-based systems are inexpensive and simple yet effective means of controlling production. They use feedback on the current situation on the shop floor to control production. They are highly visible solutions, and they do not involve any complex calculations.

Chapter 2

Basic Principles Underpinning a Card-Based Control System

Highlights

- *We outline what input/output control is.*
- *We discuss different ways in which transformed resources, transforming resources, and resource requirements can be coordinated.*
- *We outline a tool for diagnosing the stability of stations/the shop floor: the throughput diagram.*
- *We highlight the difference between planned workload/shop floor workload and, consequently, between lead time/shop floor throughput time.*

Later in this book, we will explore four card-based control systems: *kanban*, constant work-in-process (ConWIP), paired-cell overlapping loops of cards with authorization (POLCA), and control of balance by card-based navigation (COBACABANA). In this chapter, we will focus on what all four of these systems have in common. In other words, we will clarify the general principles that underpin card-based control systems—input/output control and inventory reduction.

Input/Output Control

There are two main principles underpinning all four card-based systems:

1. *The principle of input/output control*: This looks to stabilize the quantity of work that flows through the shop floor.
2. *The principle of inventory reduction*: To reduce the quantity of work on the shop floor (i.e. the work-in-process or WIP level).

Timeout: Anytime that work-in-process is not immediately transformed by a transforming resource, it is waste. We learned earlier in the book that this might be obvious waste—which can simply be eliminated—or buffer waste. In order to reduce work-in-process that functions as a buffer, the flow through the shop floor first needs to be stabilized by input/output control (or more generally by utilizing Lean tools). So the first main principle listed normally precedes the second principle.

These principles relate closely to the idea of a stable shop floor/station. So let's define a stable shop floor and a stable station.

Stable Shop Floor

A shop floor is considered stable if the input of work to the shop floor equals the output of work from the shop floor over a certain time interval.

Stable Station

Similarly, a station is considered stable if the input of work equals the output.

Timeout: According to our definition of a process—as what the product/ service experiences—an operation (process) cannot actually be stable. An operation could, for example, be to read this timeout (in the process of read-ing this book). The only thing that can be stable is the transforming resource. In this case, that is YOU who is reading this timeout (book). We can say that you are stable if the number of timeouts (or books) you finish is equal to the number of timeouts (or books) you start. As mentioned before, our separation between transforming resources and location is somewhat blurred. In our definition of a stable shop floor, we see the shop floor as an aggregated trans-forming resource.

In the first case, i.e. the stable shop floor, there will be a stable level of work on the whole shop floor. In the second case, the work waiting in front of a station to be processed is stabilized. A stable shop floor does not necessarily imply stable stations; for example, a shop floor with two stations may always have a work-in-process of 10 orders (and thus be stable), but sometimes all 10 orders queue at the first station, and sometimes all 10 orders queue at the second station. But if all stations have a stable level of work, then the shop floor is considered stable.

Being stable is, however, not enough. The process executed on the shop floor should of course be both efficient and effective.

Efficient Process

A process is considered efficient if the flow of transformed resources (the product/service flow) has zero transportation, inventory, and defect waste. An efficient process is different from an efficient transforming resource, which has zero unnecessary motion, waiting, and overproduction waste.

Effective Process

A process is considered effective if the output is equal to the resource requirements. In other words, the product/service that comes out of the process is the product/service that should come out. This means that it is neither inferior nor superior. A superior product/service can also be considered wasteful as it involves overprocessing.

This difference can be paraphrased as "Efficiency is doing the thing right and effectiveness is doing the right thing"—a famous saying accredited to Peter Drucker (a consultant who made major contributions to the practical development of management). For example, one can have an efficient air conditioning system because it has a high efficiency rating of converting hot air into cool air; but it is not effective if it doesn't cool below 75°F.

Timeout: There is no 100% efficient or effective process in reality. But this "ideal type" (Weber 2014) of a process is the only one we can define. Imagine if we were to say "almost zero" or "approaches zero." Ask two people what is meant by this expression—in measurable quantities—and you will rarely get two similar answers. An effective/efficient process is an ideal state that provides a benchmark for measuring your process. The less waste, the more efficient/effective you are.

So coordination should consider two criteria: a stable level of work on the shop floor; and the efficiency/effectiveness of the process that is executed on the shop floor. In his seminal work on organizational action, Thompson (1967) stated that there are three types of coordination: coordination by standardization, coordination by plan, and coordination by mutual adjustment.

Coordination by Standardization

This would standardize the resource requirements and create standardized transformed resources and transforming resources in such a way that all three variables are synchronized. In the Lean literature, this is referred to as standard work.

Coordination by standardization is a major Lean tool. In fact, if resource requirements are standardized, transformed and transforming resources can be standardized to achieve coordination. This is a major idea underpinning mass production. If a production line always produces the same quantity of the same product, then material (transformed resources) and capacity (transforming resources) can be fine-tuned so as to achieve a perfect match.

Coordination by Plan

This would take the resource requirements (which are considered to be known) and schedule the transformed resources and transforming resources in such a way that certain performance measures are met. These performance measures are things like the make-span (or time it takes to produce a certain set of products).

Coordination by standardization and coordination by plan are interrelated. In fact also for coordination by standardization, a plan must be devised. The main difference for us is whether resource requirements are standardized or not. In the latter case, coordination by plan, a new plan must be devised each time the resource requirements change. Coordination by plan is what underpins material requirements planning (MRP) logic, scheduling (optimization), etc. Coordination by plan constantly devises and revises a plan but does not check whether the plan is actually realized (this would be considered mutual adjustment—see the next subsection). Once a plan is devised, work is pushed through—this is why these systems are often referred to as "push systems." Consequently, coordination by plan depends on very accurate information, which is not the strength of most MRP systems in practice today. When information is not accurate, actions will be detached from reality, which may lead to severe consequences.

Timeout: Only coordination by standardization will achieve perfect coordination and allow for zero waste! Since resource requirements are standardized, transformed resources and transforming resources can be standardized to achieve this objective. For coordination by plan, this is not the case. If there is variability then there will always be some form of buffer waste, even if all variability is well known beforehand (i.e. not uncertain). This is why there are so many competing approaches for optimization/scheduling; if zero waste would be possible, all of these approaches would lead to the same results, which they rarely do—even though demand is assumed to be known beforehand.

Coordination by Mutual Adjustment

This uses communication (i.e. the exchange of information) between resource requirements, transformed resources, and transforming resources to ensure certain performance criteria, such as lead times, inventory levels, and tardiness performance, etc. are met.

Coordination by mutual adjustment is what card-based control systems do. This is based on feeding back information. It is akin to establishing a cybernetic cycle, like in a thermostat. The thermostat is the feedback to the heating, ventilation, and air conditioning (HVAC) system to provide (trigger the start of) cooling or heating as necessary. Another example is given in Figure 2.1. The water level in the bathtub is kept stable by controlling the input of water in accordance with the rate at which water is leaving the tub.

The three types of coordination and associated control solutions are summarized in Table 2.1. The coordination mechanism depends on the

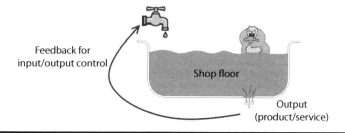

Figure 2.1 A simple control cycle—to keep the water level stable, new water only enters (input) if water leaves (output).

Table 2.1 The Three Types of Coordination and Associated Control Solutions

Coordination By	Characteristics of Resource Requirements	Control Solution	Advantage/ Disadvantage
Standardization	Resource requirements are standardized.	No specific solution. Standard work— one plan is devised and transformed, transforming resources are standardized to meet standardized resource requirements.	Simplest, most effective in terms of waste reduction. The shop floor needs to be protected from the environment—i.e. also the customer.
Plan	Resource requirements are variable.	Scheduling (optimization). Material requirements planning (MRP).	Allows transformed/ transforming resources to be optimized for a given set of resource requirements. Very sensitive to uncertainty.
Mutual adjustment	Resource requirements are uncertain.	A control cycle based on feedback loops is established.	Copes with uncertainty. Not necessarily the (or an) optimum.

variability/uncertainty of the resource requirements. This is a consequence of the law of requisite variety (Ashby 1957), which states that the variability (or flexibility) of the control solution must be equal to or greater than the variability of the system being controlled. Similarly, the responsiveness of the control solution should be equal to or greater than the uncertainty inherent to the system being controlled.

Timeout: Coordination by standardization is the best way to eliminate waste. For example, it may be the only way to realize one-piece flow with low levels of other wastes, such as waiting (one-piece flow can always be achieved by increasing capacity, but this will lead to waiting waste). It is also quite simple since only one plan is needed. So you may rightly ask why one would need coordination by plan or by mutual adjustment? But ask yourself—do you

*want to be a standardized resource requirement? You probably are famil-
iar with the experience of calling a support hotline and all they have are
standardized FAQs and answers, which you could have just looked up on
the Internet. Or imagine you are going to a hospital and your disease is not
standard. Or you want to eat pizza without pepperoni! This was Henry Ford's
original approach—"Any customer can have a car painted any color that he
wants so long as it is black" (Ford 1923, p. 71).*

All card-based control systems use coordination by mutual adjustment.
They establish a feedback loop between output and input—where the output of work determines the input of work. Since it is the output rate that
pulls work onto the shop floor, these systems are often referred to as pull
systems. An "ideal type" of pull system is a system that always has the same
amount of work entering and leaving the system.

Input/Output Control System

An input/output control system is a system in which the output determines
the input. This means a feedback loop is required, whereby the input rate
is adjusted to keep pace with the output rate and vice versa. All card-based
control systems are input/output control systems. Input/output control has
been popularized by Wight (1970) and Plossl and Wight (1971).

In other words, input/output control systems align the input and output of
work. There are two ways of achieving this:

1. By adjusting the output of the station/shop floor, e.g. by increasing
   capacity in line with the input.
2. By controlling the input to the station/shop floor.

Card-based control systems control the input of work to the shop floor/
station. This means that work is not directly released upon arrival but held
back—either at the first station of a process (*kanban*, ConWIP, and POLCA) or in
a so-called pre-shop order pool (COBACABANA). This is illustrated in Figure 2.2.

Pool

Card-based systems do not directly release orders to the shop floor. Orders
have to wait to be released. The place where orders wait is called the pool.

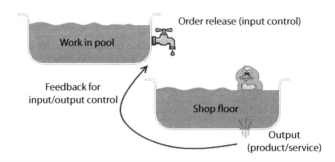

Figure 2.2   An order release system.

For us, all card-based control systems at least implicitly use a pool—this may be the first station of a process (*kanban*, ConWIP, and POLCA) or a so-called pre-shop order pool (COBACABANA).

Work is released from the pool according to the output rate. The information on the output rate is provided by means of a feedback loop; and this stabilizes the level of work-in-process.

Timeout: The concept of a pool is extremely important. The basic idea of all card-based systems is that work that is not needed should not be on the shop floor. So they withhold this work and only release it once it is required. If the work is not on the shop floor it has to be somewhere. This "somewhere" is either the pool or the queue of the first station in the process (which then functions as the pool). The work waiting in the pool/at the first station may be either transformed resources or just resource requirements in the form of order sheets, etc.

All card-based systems control the release of work to the shop floor/stations. This is achieved by setting a limit on the work allowed, which is called a work-in-process cap (WIP-Cap).

Order Release (Load-Limited)

Order release methods control the input of work to the shop floor. This is achieved by withholding work in a pool and selectively releasing work. Load-limited release methods only release work if it fits a so-called WIP-Cap.

WIP-Cap

This is the maximum amount of work-in-process allowed in a feedback loop. According to the length of the feedback loop, this may be the maximum amount at one station or across a series of stations.

The WIP-Cap is illustrated in Figure 2.3. If there is a feedback loop between Station A (or the pool) and the inventory waiting to be processed at Station B, and the WIP-Cap is three jobs, then no more than three jobs can be in the loop. In other words, if three jobs are in the loop, then it is only if a job is processed at Station B and leaves the loop that Station A is able to start working on a new job, which would then enter this loop.

Timeout: The WIP-Cap is the reason why you sometimes have to line up when visiting a bar/night club. There is typically a maximum number of people allowed inside at one time, e.g. due to fire regulations—the WIP-Cap. If this limit is reached, people have to wait outside the bar. Only if a person leaves can a new person enter the bar.

For the system to work, and to maximize profitability, the bar's bouncer/ security controlling the entrance needs feedback on how many people have left the bar (real-time, at the time they leave). This is a typical pull system. If the feedback is not real-time, they may lose revenue because people that leave are not being immediately replaced (even if someone is waiting outside the bar).

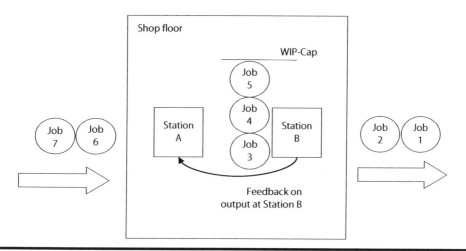

Figure 2.3   An example of a WIP-Cap between two stations.

In a push system, there is no feedback loop. The bouncer may, for example, just keep shoving people in through the front door when he/she thinks that the maximum number has not been reached until literally no one can move. At this point, if the fire marshal comes, the bar would lose its license.

A card-based control system would provide each person with a payment card that they receive at the door when they enter and that they give back when they leave (and can load and unload with credit). Controlling the number of available payment cards is a simple mechanism to control and maximize, in this case, the number of people enjoying a drink.

If the work on the shop floor is limited by the WIP-Cap, then work can only enter if work leaves the shop floor. This realizes the first principle of input/output control and stabilizes the work in the system. Meanwhile, the WIP-Cap can (and should) be lowered to reduce the work-in-process and realize the second principle. This second principle is a step toward ensuring that only the work needed is on the shop floor. However, just realizing our two principles, thereby stabilizing and reducing the work on the shop floor and/or at stations, is not enough. The new work that is released to the shop floor should also be the most urgent work (from that available to choose between in the pool) so that processes are effective. In other words, it is important to ensure that the delivery time allowance or lead time can be met. This will be explored further in Chapter 3.

Timeout: An effective process is a process that fulfills the resource requirements (i.e. what the customer wants) in all aspects—e.g. quality, delivery time, product/service features, etc. But aspects such as quality are outside the scope of card-based control systems. Thus, effectiveness for the card-based control system is mainly defined in terms of the on-time delivery performance of the product/service.

Visualizing the Stability of the Shop Floor/ Station: The Throughput Diagram

Achieving a stable level of work in front of each station is a major objective for input/output control. Whether this objective is actually being met can best be established with the help of a so-called input/output curve or throughput diagram (e.g. Conway et al. 1967; Wiendahl 1995).

Throughput Diagram

A throughput diagram gives the cumulative input and output of work to a transforming resource (e.g. a station or surgeon) or set of transforming resources (e.g. a shop floor, hospital, or bar). It allows for observing the flow of work through the transforming resource (or set of transforming resources) over time.

The throughput diagram represents an important extension compared to process flowcharts or value stream maps, which are based on a snapshot in time or on historical averages. For example, a shop floor may have an average work-in-process of 5 days when observed over a whole year. But, in certain weeks, there may have been a peak demand, e.g. where the work-in-process increases to 20 days while for the rest of the time it is actually only 3 days. The throughput diagram makes these fluctuations, which are hidden by aggregate data and averages, visible; and it allows for problem diagnosis.

Moreover, process flowcharts and value stream maps naturally only focus on processes. Yet we saw earlier in this chapter that a "stable process" is not a meaningful concept. Rather, what is meant is that the level of work at each station (transforming resource) or the shop floor (set of transforming resources) is stable. Creating a mix of processes (i.e. products/services) that smoothens or levels the work across stations is a key to input/output control. Remember, achieving a stable level of work is the objective, and this can be made visible by the throughput diagram.

The throughput diagram consists of curves, which represent the cumulative work that enters and exits the shop floor and/or a particular station. This is why the curves in a throughput diagram are also called input and output curves. Time is on the horizontal X-axis while cumulative work is on the vertical Y-axis. Work can be measured in any unit, e.g. processing time, service time, patients, or even slices of pizza.

In order to create a throughput diagram, let's first create a cumulative input curve. As soon as new work arrives, it is added to the cumulative input curve. This is illustrated in Figure 2.4.

Now let's create a cumulative output curve. This is similar to the cumulative input curve but lagged in time—as soon as previously inputted work is complete, it is added to the output curve. Both curves (the input and the output curve) constitute the basic throughput diagram, as depicted in Figure 2.5.

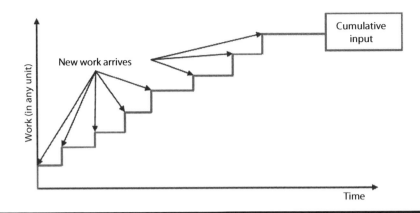

Figure 2.4   Creating an input curve.

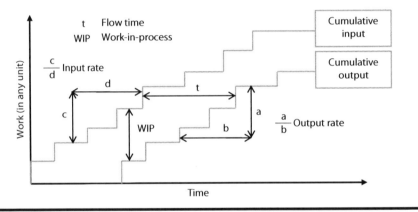

Figure 2.5   A basic throughput diagram (input/output curve).

The work currently in the system is the work that entered the system minus the work that left the system. Therefore, it follows that the work-in-process is given by the vertical distance between the input and output curves. Similarly, the horizontal distance indicates the time that work stays in the system. Finally, the realized input and output rate—i.e. the rate at which work enters the system and leaves the system—is visualized by the inclination or gradient of the curves. This reflects a basic law in operations management: Little's Law (Little 1961). This law states that, in a stable system—i.e. where the input and output curves are parallel or keep pace with each other in the long run—the average flow time is given by the work-in-process divided by the average throughput rate.

Timeout: You may know Little's Law stated differently as:

$$\text{Work-in-process} = \text{throughput rate} \times \text{time in the system}$$

We have transformed the equation to reflect time as being the result of (or caused by) the level of work-in-process and the throughput rate. Time is always realized! It cannot be directly influenced but can only be affected by influencing the level of work-in-process and/or the throughput rate. Little's Law is important since it relates work-in-process to time.

For many companies, the objective of performance improvement is not primarily to reduce inventory but to reduce flow time (i.e. to increase delivery speed and responsiveness). You cannot have one without the other (except by increasing the output rate). Also, note that Little's Law is based on average values. Reducing the level of work-in-process may reduce the flow time for the majority of jobs, but it may delay some specific jobs, which may be very important to the company and to its customer.

Temporarily overloaded or under-loaded resources can now easily be identified from the throughput diagram (see Figure 2.6). In overload periods, inventory waste is created since transformed resources have to wait for transforming resources, and flow times increase; in under-load periods, waiting waste is introduced. Smoothing the work by shifting appropriate parts of the workload from overloaded to under-loaded periods can therefore be a major key to performance improvements.

Timeout: The simplest way to smooth the workload is by introducing a pool of work. We will see later in the chapter that this is how card-based control systems stabilize work on the shop floor. However, this does not apply at the higher level where work is acquired, i.e. sales. To avoid under-load periods, many companies use an "overbooking" strategy (e.g. airlines) or react to under-load periods using sales promotions. But this may lead to unwanted overload periods since, for example, sales are at the reduced promotional

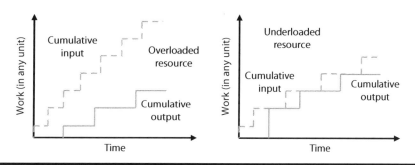

Figure 2.6   Identifying overloaded and underloaded resources in the throughput diagram.

price. An alternative solution is letting the actual competitive capabilities of the firm drive the competitiveness of the bid and thus the probability that an order is won. For example, Thürer et al. (2014) recently showed that a delivery time allowance that reflects a firm's actual operational capabilities allows the firm's workload to be stabilized. For example, when the workload increases, available capacity reduces, and the delivery times offered to customers become longer. This reduces the probability that a company will win an order. But as the workload gradually decreases, available capacity increases and shorter, more competitive delivery times can be offered, which reduces the lead times that can be quoted and increases the order-winning probability. This smoothens or balances the workload over time. Alternatively, shorter delivery times can be offered by increasing capacity, but the cost of extra capacity should be reflected in the price, which in turn reduces order-winning probability thereby establishing the same smoothing cycle as above.

We often observe in practice that companies take the order no matter what—but this is not a good strategy if, from the outset, the promised delivery time is not realizable or the costs incurred to achieve the delivery time (e.g. the cost of overtime) far exceed the price. In both cases—nothing will be gained but a lot may be lost.

Recovering from a temporary overload period also makes the waiting buffer waste visible. This is illustrated in Figure 2.7. A steep inclination during the recovery period shows that the transforming resource is able to increase the output rate. This is the capacity of the transforming resource that is, on average, not used—i.e. it is waiting waste. It is buffer waiting waste since it is used to buffer the system against the increase in input (i.e. variability).

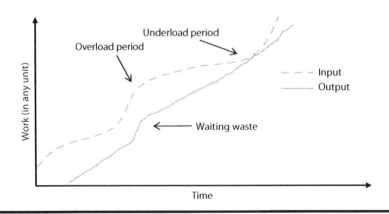

Figure 2.7   The appearance of waiting waste in the throughput diagram.

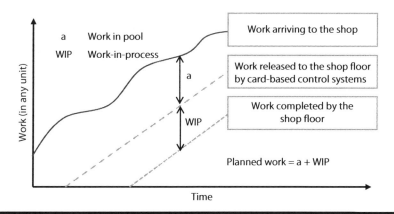

Figure 2.8   The basic idea underlying card-based control systems, illustrated using a throughput diagram.

Reducing this waiting waste will create inventory waste—as is visible from the input/output curves. Thus, it is a buffer by our definition.

The basic idea underlying card-based control systems is to stabilize and reduce work-in-process. This can now be illustrated using a throughput diagram (see Figure 2.8). Card-based control systems use an order release mechanism to divide the work accepted by the shop as a whole (the planned work) into (i) the work on the shop floor (the released work or work-in-process); and (ii) the work in the pool (the unreleased work).

The difference between planned workload and work-in-process is important. So let's define both concepts:

Work-in-Process (Released Work)

The work currently released to the shop floor (queuing or being processed at a station on the shop floor).

Planned Work

All work accepted by the shop that is to be processed. This is the work-waiting to be released (i.e. the work in the pool) and the work-in-process released to the shop floor.

If jobs are released immediately, and are therefore not withheld from the shop floor, the planned work and work-in-process will be identical. But if order release is applied, the work-in-process becomes a subset of the

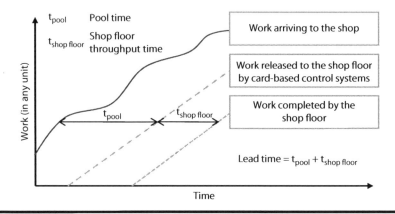

Figure 2.9   The composition of the (realized) lead time.

planned work. Order release controls the flow of orders from the pool onto the shop floor to stabilize the work-in-process, not the planned work. It protects the shop floor from fluctuations in the planned workload. The planned workload is controlled through the sales/bidding function, as discussed in the previous timeout.

All three workloads—the planned workload, pool workload, and work-in-process—released to the shop floor relate to a certain proportion of the time that work spends in the system. The following time-based measures can be identified (see also Figure 2.9):

Lead Time

This is the time that work spends in the whole system, i.e. the shop. It is the sum of the pool time and the shop floor throughput time (see below).

Pool Time

This is the time that work spends in front of the shop floor (or at the first station) waiting to be released.

Shop Floor Throughput Time

This is the time that work spends on the shop floor. It is the sum of the operation throughput times for each station in the routing of a job.

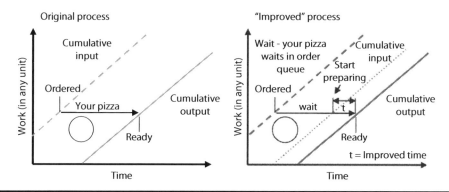

Figure 2.10   An example of the difference between the shop floor throughput time and lead time.

Operation throughput times consist of processing times, set-up times, and queuing times.

Timeout: The time-based measures illustrate an important fact: most card-based control systems only stabilize the work, and thus the flow time, on the shop floor. But in certain control problems, the customer experiences the whole lead time (e.g. the pool time plus the shop floor throughput time).

For example, imagine you order a pizza, and they tell you that they reduced the time to make your pizza from 1 hour to 10 minutes. But what they didn't tell you is that your pizza now has to wait 50 minutes in the customer order queue before even entering the process! In the end, how would you feel? We think we know the answer.

If the output rate is not improved (e.g. by eliminating waiting waste, unnecessary motion, etc.), then the number of pizzas coming out per hour remains the same. The only thing that changes is where the pizza waits—not the total lead time experienced by the customer (see Figure 2.10).

So, in the end, it doesn't help you that they reduced the throughput time from 1 hour to 10 minutes. Therefore, what is so positive about card-based control systems? Well, here are some answers:

■ *Inventory is reduced (so, in this example, ingredients remain fresh);*
■ *Design changes (e.g. gorgonzola rather than cheddar cheese) can easily be accommodated while the product (pizza) waits in the pool; and*

■ *Products (pizzas) can easily be prioritized—e.g. if an important customer comes in and they really need the pizza in 10 minutes, they can have it in 10 minutes.*

Summary: Input/Output Control Underpinning Card-Based Control

All four card-based control systems considered in this book are based on input/output control. In other words, they control the input of work to the shop floor/stations in line with the output rate. This is achieved by establishing a so-called WIP-Cap, which is a limit on the work that is allowed to enter the shop floor. When the work that can enter the shop floor is limited, new work can only enter if work leaves the shop floor. This realizes the first principle underlying card-based systems and stabilizes the level of work-in-process on the shop floor. The WIP-Cap can be tightened, which then realizes the second principle—the reduction of work-in-process. Whether a shop floor is truly stable can be diagnosed with the help of a throughput diagram. This diagram depicts the cumulative input and output of work to a transforming resource or a set of transforming resources.

Regulating the input of work in line with the output rate has two structural consequences that are shared by all four card-based systems:

1. Work is not directly released to the shop floor but has to wait to be released to the shop floor. Hence, all four systems create a so-called pool where work awaits its release. This may be an explicit pool or just the queue at the first station in the process. This pool may consist of work on paper or be physical in the form of materials, patients, etc.
2. Feedback on the output rate needs to be provided (so that further inputs can be released). Thus, all four card-based systems establish feedback loops. We will see that the way that these loops are realized (in terms of who provides feedback to whom and information transmitted by the cards) determines the applicability of each system to a given control problem.

We also saw that input/output control does not necessarily create a more effective or efficient process or set of processes. A card-based control system can only be considered efficient if it reduces wastes, e.g. by balancing the workload across resources. Meanwhile, a card-based control system can be considered effective if it ensures a product/service is provided on time. Therefore, the work waiting in the pool and on the shop floor should be sequenced or considered in accordance with some measure of urgency, such as earliest delivery date. This will be discussed in the next chapter.

Highlights Revisited

- *We outline what input/output control is.* The simplest way to realize stable stations (the transforming resources) is to align the input of work with the output of work. This is called input/output control and is the first principle of all card-based systems discussed in this book. The second principle refers to constantly trying to reduce the work-in-process in the system.

- *We discuss different ways in which transformed resources, transforming resources, and resource requirements can be coordinated.* Coordination can be by standardization, by plan, or by mutual adjustment. Coordination by standardization (standard work) is what most Lean approaches do. Transformed/transforming resources are standardized in accordance with standardized resource requirements. Coordination by plan is what most scheduling and optimization based approaches (e.g. MRP) do. A plan is devised that coordinates transformed/transforming resources and resource requirements. Since resource requirements are not standardized, perfect coordination is unlikely to occur. Moreover, each time something changes, a new plan needs to be devised. Coordination by plan does not take any feedback into account on whether or not anticipated future situations are actually realized—once a plan is devised, it is pushed through. Meanwhile, feedback on the current situation is used by coordination by mutual adjustment. This is the type of coordination that card-based control systems use. They use feedback on the current output to control the input of work to the system.

- *We outline a tool for diagnosing the stability of stations/the shop floor—the throughput diagram.* The throughput diagram depicts the cumulative input and output of work from a transforming resource (or a set of transforming resources) over time. This illustrates Little's Law; and it allows workload fluctuations over time to be visualized.

■ *We highlight the difference between planned workload/shop floor workload and, consequently, lead time/shop floor throughput time.* Card-based control systems withhold work that is not needed from the shop floor. This separates the work in the system into the shop floor workload and the pool load(i.e. the work waiting to be released in the pool); with the planned workload given by the sum of both. Consequently, there are two different flow times: the lead time from acceptance by the shop to completion (which is linked to the planned workload); and the shop floor throughput time (which is linked to the stabilized work-in-process on the shop floor). More often than not, the customer experiences the total lead time rather than the shop floor throughput time—hence, this is important.

Chapter 3

Simplified Scheduling through Pool Sequencing and a Shop Floor Dispatching Rule

Highlights

- *We outline how a simplified form of scheduling is realized through the use of pool sequencing and dispatching rules.*
- *We outline a set of simple yet effective dispatching rules for use on the shop floor.*
- *We outline a tool for diagnosing the performance of the pool sequencing and dispatching rule known as the order progress diagram.*

Card-based control systems create a stable shop floor and/or stable stations. This is different from an efficient/effective process. A stable shop floor/station means that the work that goes in is equal to the work that comes out. But it is also possible that the work that enters and leaves the system may be work that is not needed at all (or an order that is not needed yet). If we are not careful, the order that is really needed may stay in the pool or on the shop floor forever. For example, an operator may not like the operation needed for this order and may just process all other work he/she has available; or he/she may select the work first that gives him/her the highest bonus—this is called cherry-picking. So what we need is a rule for sequencing work/orders in the pool and a rule for determining how orders are dispatched or processed on the shop floor (see Figure 3.1). This will help

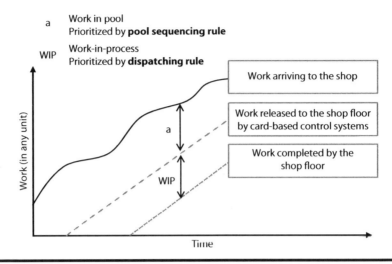

Figure 3.1   The function of the pool sequencing and shop floor dispatching rules.

to ensure operators are working on the right orders at the right time to meet the objectives of the shop.

Pool Sequencing Rule (Pre-Shop Floor)

Determines the priority of the work that is in the pool waiting to be released to the shop floor.

Dispatching Rule (Shop Floor)

If more than one job is waiting in front of a station to be processed (i.e. if two or more jobs are competing for the same resource), then a decision has to be made regarding which job to process next. This is what we call the dispatching decision. This decision may follow a rule, which we call the dispatching rule. Dispatching rules can be very sophisticated or very straightforward rules, like first-in-first-out (FIFO).

Pool sequencing and dispatching rules represent a simplified form of scheduling. Scheduling, as used for "coordination by plan," determines when an operation must take place; so a basic assumption is that the schedule is adhered to. On the other hand, pool sequencing and dispatching rules use priority measures for "coordination by mutual adjustment." While these rules may also schedule a planned release date and a set of operation due dates, these dates are just used for prioritization.

For example, when we schedule a release date for an order at Friday noon, then the order is released at Friday noon. Meanwhile, with a pool sequencing rule, the order may be released at any time as soon; for example, it may be released earlier since capacity suddenly became available (and it is the most urgent order) or later since a machine broke down and work is piling up, or because there is a more urgent order waiting. So, for the pool sequencing rule, the actual release can be driven by a different measure—i.e. the current workload on the shop floor. This allows for combining input/output control with the effective timing of release decisions. For scheduling, the order would be released at Friday noon regardless of the current load situation on the shop floor. This is why a high level of information accuracy on the future state of a system is needed for this kind of coordination by plan (i.e. scheduling).

Timeout: We recently worked with a small assembly shop. Different parts had to be produced at the same set of transforming resources before they were assembled at an assembly station. A major challenge was how to ensure that the parts that made up a final assembly arrived at the assembly station at the same time. This can be achieved by determining an assembly due date. A planned release date and a set of operation due dates are then scheduled from this assembly due date for each part that makes up the assembly order. The progress of parts toward the assembly station can then be synchronized using the planned release dates for prioritization in the pool (at release) and the set of operation due dates for prioritizing order progress on the shop floor—even in high-variety contexts.

Some Rules for Priority Dispatching on the Shop Floor

FIFO, also known as first-come-first-served (FCFS), is one of the most commonly applied dispatching rules in practice. For example, Monden (1983, p. 25) reported that, at Toyota, workers should follow the sequence in which *kanbans* arrived at a process, i.e. first-in-first-out. Indeed, many practitioners use the FIFO rule to overcome negative behavior such as the cherry-picking phenomenon described previously in this chapter.

First-In-First-Out (FIFO)

The job that arrived at the station first is processed next.

Timeout: There are physical restrictions that may automatically enforce a dispatching rule. For example, a pile of work may only allow for taking the last in first. This rule would then be last-in-first-out. While material may not complain about this kind of priority, customers can talk and typically will! This may require a redesign of the physical environment to allow for the use of different dispatching rules.

FIFO is arguably the best rule if orders have no delivery dates and the variability of processing times is low. However, it is a poor choice of dispatching rule if a due date has been agreed and/or there is processing time variability. First, if there exists processing time variability, some form of load balancing is required. Second, if there exists a delivery or due date, the FIFO rule does not necessarily ensure good due date adherence. Rather, a due date oriented dispatching rule should be used. The simplest due date oriented dispatching rule is the earliest due date (EDD) rule.

Earliest Due Date (EDD)

The job with the earliest due date is processed first.

Timeout: Imagine two customers phone to place orders for pizza. The first customer orders a pizza and wants it delivered locally in an hour; the second customer calls 5 minutes later and wants to come in and pick up a pizza in 15 minutes. Under FIFO, the first pizza would receive priority although the second pizza is the most urgent. EDD would prioritize the most urgent pizza.

EDD is a powerful due date oriented dispatching rule suitable for many environments. But imagine you have orders that require only one or two operations and orders that require many operations; and the due date does not depend on the number of operations. So, one job has only one operation and has to be delivered in 10 days, while the other has six operations and has to be delivered in 11 days. EDD would select the first order. Wouldn't it be smarter to select the second order? A rule that considers the number of operations and operation throughput times is the operation due date (ODD) rule.

Operation Due Date (ODD)

The job with the earliest operation due date is processed first. The operation due date is calculated by backward scheduling from the production due date

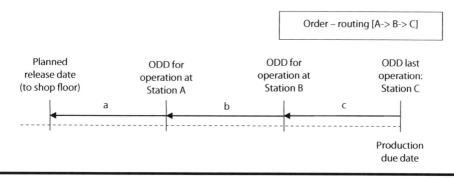

Figure 3.2   Determination of operation due dates for shop floor dispatching. Planned operation throughput time at Stations A, a; B, b; and C, c.

(see Figure 3.2). The ODD of the last operation in the routing is equal to the production due date. The planned release date is the date when the order should be released to the shop floor. It is used for the pool sequencing decision, i.e. to decide the sequence in which orders are considered for release to the shop floor. This is similar to the logic inherent to material requirements planning.

Timeout: When card-based systems are applied, planned operation throughput times are typically considered to be constant. This is possible since they are stabilized by the card-based control system. If a station is stable then, according to Little's Law, the average operation throughput time is also stable. This constant may contain the processing time or just account for the waiting time. The operation throughput time is the processing time plus the time the job spends in the queue waiting to be processed—the waiting time. Finally, you may wonder about the term "production due date." The production due date is the customer due date minus an allowance for the variance of lateness. You will encounter it again in Chapter 9 and specifically in Figure 9.2.

The above due date setting rules are all oriented around some measure of time. However, there are other rules that focus on the workload, i.e. rules that are load-oriented rather than being time-oriented. These rules are often not applied together with card-based systems since it is assumed that the card-based system already stabilizes and reduces the workload on the shop floor. However, they can play a major role in contexts where there is high variety in processing times. The simplest load-oriented rule is the shortest processing time (SPT) rule.

Shortest Processing Time (SPT)

The job with the shortest processing time is processed first.

The SPT rule plays an important role in avoiding starvation or idleness caused by high processing time variability. Starvation at a station is postponed by giving priority to jobs with the shortest processing times at upstream stations since this will create the quickest replenishment of successive queues. Of course, this presupposes that only work that is needed is on the shop floor. Otherwise, SPT may just create more overproduction waste. As mentioned previously, an idle transforming resource may be a "bad" thing (in the case that there are customer requirements for this resource), a "good" thing (in the case that there are no customer requirements, i.e. to avoid overproduction, capacity could be used in another way, e.g. to perform maintenance tasks), or "normal" (since a utilization level of 90%, for example, implies a waiting of 10%).

In general, SPT is a rule that should be applied with care since it completely neglects the urgency of work. An alternative dispatching rule, which combines the advantages of ODD and SPT dispatching, i.e. time-oriented (due date) and load-oriented rules, is the modified operation due dates (MODD) rule.

Modified Operation Due Date (MODD)

The MODD rule prioritizes jobs according to a lowest priority number, which is given by the maximum of the operation due date and earliest finish time. The earliest finish time is given by the time when the dispatching decision is made plus the processing time.

So, under MODD, if jobs are on time, they are prioritized according to the ODD rule—since the operation due date is higher than the earliest finish time, the priority number for all jobs will be the operation due date. But if jobs become tardy, they are prioritized according to the SPT rule, since now the earliest finishing time is higher than the operation due date. The MODD rule shifts between a focus on ODDs to complete jobs on time and a focus on speeding up jobs (through SPT) when multiple jobs exceed their ODD. MODD is more complex than the other rules described; but, if it can be applied, it is the best choice for complex environments, e.g. with high processing time and routing variability. Finally, the five dispatching rules discussed are summarized in Table 3.1.

Table 3.1   Summary of Dispatching Rules Discussed

Name of Dispatching Rule	Short Description	Comment
FIFO (first-in-first-out) or FCFS (first-comes-first-served)	Simple time-based rule for inventory control problem i.e. no due date.	Is outperformed by EDD (see below) if there is a due date.
EDD (earliest due date)	Simple time-based rule if orders have a due date. The job with the earliest due date is processed first.	Is outperformed by ODD (see below) if orders have differing routing lengths (or operation throughput times) from which the due date is independent.
ODD (operation due dates)	Time-based rule that calculates an operation due date for each operation. The job with the earliest operation due date is processed first.	Requires some (simple) calculations.
SPT (shortest processing time)	Simple load-based rule. The job with the shortest processing time is processed first.	Significantly reduces average throughput times and consequently average lateness. Reduces starvation at downstream stations, especially if routing is directed. However, neglects the urgency of jobs, which may result in high tardiness for large jobs.
MODD (modified operation due date)	Prioritizes orders according to the lowest priority number, which is given by the maximum of the operation due date and earliest finish time (which is the current time plus the processing time).	The MODD rule shifts between a focus on ODDs to complete jobs on time and a focus on speeding up jobs— through SPT effects— when multiple jobs exceed their ODD.

Visualizing On-Time Performance: The Order Progress Diagram

The throughput diagram we introduced in the previous chapter allows for diagnosing input/output control, i.e. the stability of the shop floor/stations. However, we also saw that this alone is not enough; the stabilized work also has to be the right work for production control to be effective. In other words, for diagnosing production control, we also have to visualize on-time performance.

Timeout: We saw that Little's Law establishes a link between stable work-in-process on the shop floor and stable shop floor throughput times. However, Little's Law is based on the average. If you are desperately waiting for a train, it does not typically help you (as an individual passenger) when the train company tells you that, on average, they are on time. Forget the average train—you want your train to be on time!

It is therefore important not only to look at averages but also to monitor individual orders. The order progress diagram (Soepenberg et al. 2008) makes the on-time performance of individual orders visible. This allows for problem diagnosis since it shows if delivery time allowances are not appropriate, i.e. it shows if and when work becomes either tardy or too early. While being too early may not appear to be a problem, it actually means that the allowance is too long, i.e. not competitive, or that resources are being used to process the wrong orders (which results in overproduction and/or finished goods inventory waste). If you are going to pick up a pizza that you phoned to order, you don't want it ready 10 minutes before you are due to arrive. If some orders are early and some orders are late, it may be possible to redirect the shop's efforts to converge more of the orders to their promised delivery dates.

Order Progress Diagram

The order progress diagram (see Figure 3.3 for an example) depicts the order progress as a series of linked data points. Each data point gives the relative lateness for each operation of an order on the vertical axis and the realized operation completion date on the horizontal axis. The relative lateness is given by the actually realized operation

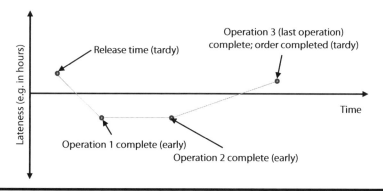

Figure 3.3 The order progress diagram.

completion time minus the expected operation completion time (or operation due date).

In an ideal situation, all dots would lie on the horizontal axis—this would mean that there is no relative lateness. In the example illustrated in Figure 3.3, there is an order with three operations. We find that the order is already tardy at release, i.e. was released later than planned. The order then speeds up during Operation 1. This means that the realized operation throughput time that the order experienced at the first station was less than the given allowance. The reason for this may be that the order was expedited to get it back on track, e.g. by an ODD dispatching rule.

If order progress is parallel to the horizontal line, as it is during Operation 2, then the realized operation throughput time and the allowance are equal. No new lateness is accumulated, but also no lateness is reduced. Finally, in the example, the order progress slows down—i.e. the given allowance is too short for the realized operation throughput time—during the last operation, resulting in an increase in lateness and, overall, an increase in the tardiness of the order.

Tracking the order progress of several orders allows for diagnosing where tardiness/earliness occurs, e.g. common problem spots may be identified. This allows for better timing decisions, and aligns the allowance with the realized operation throughput times. For example, in the pizza example given in Figure 3.4, we see that the estimate for the time in the oven was too short. If this happens repeatedly, the estimate is likely to be wrong since the cooking time should be reasonably stable. It should therefore be corrected, so the person who puts the cheese on the pizza has more time to do their job properly, etc.

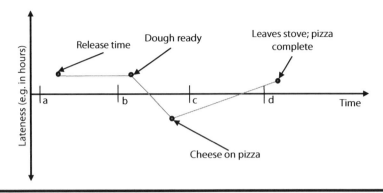

Figure 3.4 The order progress diagram—pizza example. (a) planned start your pizza; (b) planned dough ready; (c) planned cheese on pizza; (d) planned leave stove—ready.

Summary: Simplified Scheduling through Priority Dispatching

To ensure efficient and effective processes, card-based systems need not only to stabilize the work in the system but also to ensure that the right work is processed, i.e. work is completed on time. To ensure the right jobs are worked on, card-based control systems incorporate a simplified form of scheduling. Rather than determining a schedule to be adhered to in advance (i.e. coordination by plan), priority measures are used to prioritize the progress of work through the shop. This means that, for example, the decision concerning which job to process next is taken based on the priority of the jobs currently queuing at a station rather than based on some preconceived plan of which jobs would be queuing at the station. Work in the pool waiting to be released to the shop floor is prioritized by the pool sequencing rule. Work queuing in front of a station is prioritized by a shop floor dispatching rule. The effectiveness of this prioritization can be diagnosed with the help of an order progress diagram. This diagram depicts the relative lateness accumulated at each process step (operation) for each individual order.

Highlights Revisited

■ *We outline how a simplified form of scheduling is realized through the use of pool sequencing and dispatching rules.* Scheduling, as used for "coordination by plan," determines when an operation must take place; so a basic assumption is that the schedule is adhered to. On the other hand, pool sequencing and dispatching rule use priority measures for "coordination by mutual adjustment." This allows for integrating a timing component into input/output control, which aims at stable stations (a stable shop floor).

■ *We outline a set of simple yet effective dispatching rules for use on the shop floor.* Five basic rules are introduced. First-in-first-out (FIFO) is arguably the best rule if orders have no delivery dates and the variability of processing times is low since, for example, it overcomes negative worker behavior such as cherry-picking. But it may lead to prioritizing a less urgent job if jobs have individual due (or delivery) dates. In such a case, the earliest due date (EDD) rule is a better choice. But if orders also differ in terms of the number of operations required, the operation due date (ODD) rule, which determines a due date for each operation in the routing of a job by simple backward scheduling, is a better choice. Meanwhile, if there is high processing time variability, selecting the job with the shortest processing time (SPT) may lead to the best results, since it avoids starvation introduced by processing time variability. But SPT does not consider the urgency of jobs, which may lead to extreme tardiness especially for large jobs. An alternative rule that combines ODD and SPT dispatching is the modified operation due date (MODD) rule. While this rule is more sophisticated, it is arguably the best choice in practice for high-variety contexts.

■ *We outline a tool for diagnosing the performance of the pool sequencing and dispatching rule known as the order progress diagram.* The order progress diagram depicts the order progress as a series of linked data points where each data point gives the relative lateness for each operation of an order on the vertical axis and the realized operation completion date on the horizontal axis. This goes beyond the average (which can be analyzed by a throughput diagram) to the individual order. It allows for diagnosing when and where the lateness of an individual order is created.

Chapter 4

How to Diagnose a Control Problem?

Highlights

- ■ *We outline the difference between to-stock and to-order (the to-stock/to-order interface).*
- ■ *We outline the difference between customer penetration point and inventory/order separation point.*
- ■ *We outline the difference between routing and layout.*
- ■ *We discuss the different forms of variability in customer demand.*

The previous chapter explored what all card-based control systems have in common. We discovered that they all control the input of work to the shop floor in line with the output rate. This creates a stable shop floor and allows low levels of work-in-process to be realized. So far, so good; but you might now be asking yourself: if they all do the same thing, then why not just pick and use any one of them?

There are in fact significant differences between the four systems considered in this book—*kanban*, constant work-in-process (ConWIP), paired-cell overlapping loops of cards with authorization (POLCA), and control of balance by card-based navigation (COBACABANA). Each emerged in response to a different need/control problem. We will therefore now explore the main criteria on which these control problems differ—and this will allow us to diagnose where they apply or are most suitable. In much of the remainder of this book (Chapters 5 through 9), we will then reveal the mechanics

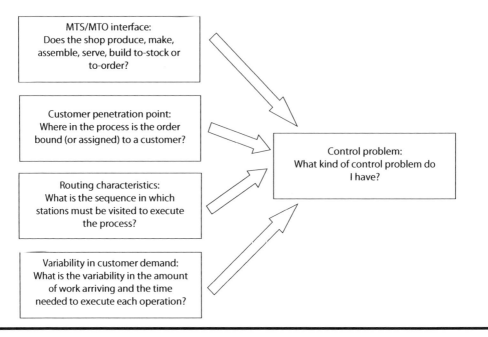

Figure 4.1   Four criteria for control problem diagnosis.

underlying card-based control systems and how these systems address the different diagnosed problems. Chapter 10 will summarize our findings.

When diagnosing a control problem, we will look at four criteria (see Figure 4.1):

1. Whether the process precedes the resource requirements (to-stock) or whether the resource requirements precede the process (to-order)? In other words, whether a shop assembles, serves, builds, etc. to-stock or to-order?
2. At what point in the process does the product/service become assigned and bound to a particular customer? In other words, where is the customer penetration point?
3. What are the characteristics of the sequence in which stations need to be visited to execute the processes of the mix of jobs on the shop floor? In other words, what are the routing characteristics of the orders produced by the shop?
4. How variable are processing times and how sporadic are demands placed on the shop? In general, what is the variability in customer demand?

We will see that all four criteria refer to resource requirements. Card-based systems seek to coordinate the flow of transformed resources through transforming resources so that they are synchronized with the resource requirements. So the resources requirements pose a constraint on how the flow of transformed resources through transforming resources should be realized.

Timeout: Your industry, customer, and core competencies ultimately dictate what control problem you encounter and, consequently, which control solution you should apply. This should come as no surprise, yet many companies appear to neglect this fact—we had the example in Chapter 2 with the call center that has only standardized answers, the hospital that may only have treatment for a certain set of diseases, etc. In fact, a first step taken by managers when challenged by complex control problems is simplifying the control problem through the standardization of customer requirements. But although making all cars black would allow for the use of a simple conveyor belt—would it really make customers happier in the twenty-first century? For a car, a customer that wants choice will simply go to another producer—but what if we are talking about a health-care system? To provide good health care for all diseases, we need to face up to complex control problems rather than arguably taking the easy way out by seeking to simplify them.

Criterion 1: Make/Produce/Assemble/Build/ Serve, etc. To-Stock or To-Order

Here, we use the expression "to-order" and "to-stock" rather than, for example, the more commonly used "make-to-stock" and "make-to-order." It is the timing aspect (i.e. before or after demand) that is important to us. The verb before, i.e. the produced, made, served, assembled, etc., just describes the underlying process.

To-Stock

The operations (i.e. the transformation of transformed resources) occur before the resource requirements are known. Decisions are based on expected resource requirements (determined, e.g. by forecasting demand). As operations occur ahead of demand, the customer does not have to wait but also cannot easily customize the offering.

To-Order

The operations (i.e. the transformation of transformed resources) occur after the resource requirements are known. The customer is always waiting! It is just a matter of how long they wait. Because operations take place after the requirements are known, there is the possibility of customizing the product/service offering. This can best be illustrated by way of a throughput diagram, as given in Figure 4.2.

An important point that seems to contradict most of the academic literature is that we argue to-stock or to-order does not directly impact the decision concerning which control solution to choose. Rather, it only determines the boundary conditions—i.e. the waste allowance—under which the control solution can operate.

- To-stock just means that the product has left the process and is waiting for the customer (as finished goods inventory).
- To-order just means that there are still operations yet to be completed before the product/service can be delivered.

Neither case achieves perfect coordination since resource requirements are either preceded or succeeded. We saw above that only the standardization of resource requirements can achieve perfect coordination. To-order typically produces waiting waste, while to-stock typically produces overproduction and/or inventory waste.

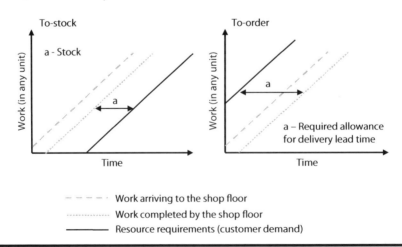

Figure 4.2 The difference between to-stock and to-order, illustrated by a throughput diagram.

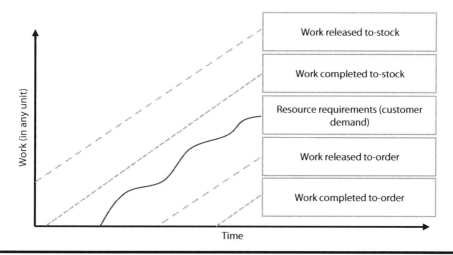

Figure 4.3 The to-stock/to-order interface, illustrated by a throughput diagram.

But this does not impact the control problem. The main impact on the control problem is that *to-order* presupposes a delivery time allowance. Since the product still has to be produced, the customer has to give an allowance for the time it takes to produce the output. In a *to-stock* system, the customer expects it to be immediately available (in stock). However, we find in reality that production/service systems are a hybrid of partially to-stock and to-order. This can allow, for example, for mass customization. The separation point is called the to-stock/to-order interface, as illustrated in Figure 4.3 using a throughput diagram.

To-Stock/To-Order Interface

The point in the process at which production awaits demand rather than precedes demand. A *to-stock* system anticipates resource requirements, while a *to-order* system reacts to resource requirements.

Timeout: If there is a stock-out in a to-stock system, it automatically turns into a to-order system—in the short term at least. In general, most companies integrate different processes where part of the system is to-stock and part is to-order. For example, the supply (i.e. stockroom) for a to-order system may be based on a to-stock system. A pharmacy may produce medicines based on a patient's prescription, but it has the materials it needs in stock. For us, what is important is that the to-stock/to-order interface determines the waiting time that the customer experiences (and is willing to experience—i.e. allows for in their own decision making).

A to-order system reacts to resource requirements while a to-stock system anticipates resource requirements. This means that a to-stock system requires a tool for predicting resource requirements—and this typically involves forecasting. But this alone is not enough, since what is actually needed is the resource requirements to start production here and now. Therefore, the forecasted demand has to be "back-scheduled" to determine the planned resource requirements for starting production. This process of forecasting and back-scheduling inherent to a to-stock system is illustrated in Figure 4.4.

Timeout: Back-scheduling is a major reason for the inaccuracies of material requirements planning (MRP) systems, as parameters (such as lead time offsets) are padded out by each department "just in case." This then creates overproduction by scheduling the start date prior to when it is really needed. Similarly, in a re-order point system (as is illustrated in Figure 4.5), the re-order point is based on forecast demand, i.e. the consumption rate and the time to replenish the inventory. The key to low inventories in a to-stock system is consequently good forecasting of demand and a stable time for replenishing stocks (to simplify back-scheduling). Card-based control systems can be an important means of achieving the latter.

This means that to-stock systems introduce two errors in terms of resource requirements: a forecasting error and a back-scheduling error. But the delivery lead time experienced by the customer is zero. To-order

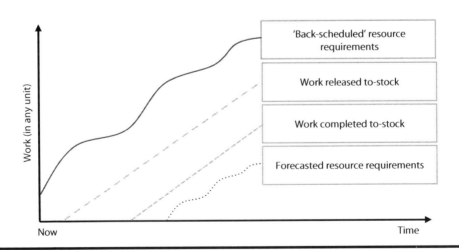

Figure 4.4 A to-stock system: Forecasting and back-scheduling to obtain resource requirements for process input.

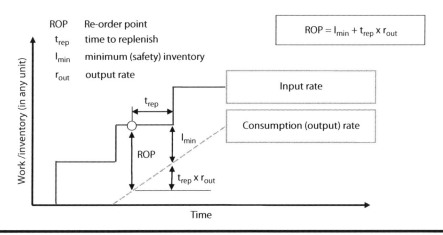

Figure 4.5   Re-order point calculation.

systems avoid both errors since the system input is determined by the actual resource requirements of the customer. But the customer has to wait for his/her product or service.

Timeout: Pizzas are typically cooked to-order since customers want them fresh and hot. They are willing to wait, at least within a certain tolerance. Imagine a pizza outlet that has the cooked pizza in stock when you arrive. They have to forecast when you go there—let's say they predict that a person will arrive at 20:00 who wants a pepperoni pizza from stock. Next, they have to "back-schedule" when to start producing the pizza. Many pizza outlets have a selection of pizzas in stock in pizza pans in the window or case; but how long have they been sitting there? This is also a problem with coffee shops that have coffee sitting out in carafes. They have to forecast when to produce the output in order to minimize the waste. How often do you get a bitter, lukewarm cup of coffee because it has been sitting there for hours? Starbucks, however, has timers on its coffee so, when the timer goes off, they make a new pot. In an effort to minimize waste, they also stop making decaf coffee outside certain hours of the day, which converts it from a to-stock to a to-order system where they make it "Americana style," and you have to wait for it.

Criterion 2: The Customer Penetration (Inventory/Order Separation) Point

Each process has a customer penetration point and an inventory/order separation point. These two points are different from the to-stock/to-order interface, which just captures the time component of demand—in other words, whether operations (i.e. the transformation of transformed resources) precedes the resource requirements or not. Although in practice all three often overlap, is it important to distinguish between all three, since they capture different aspects of a process. The customer penetration point is the point where an order becomes destined for or assigned to a particular customer. The inventory/order separation point is the point where an order becomes uniquely identified by the production control system. Both involve the concept of identity. So let's set this concept straight first.

Identity

In a simplified form (without going into philosophical discussions), the term "identity" tells us something about what characterizes a person, product, service, etc. If two objects have all of the same characteristics or properties in common, then they are identical, the same, or selfsame.

Genidentity

This is a concept originally introduced by Kurt Lewin, one of the founders of social psychology. It extends the common identity concept. Genidentity means that an object maintains its "identity" during a change process. One object is genidentical to another because it developed from this object. In other words—a tree is genidentical to the seed it grew from (although both are not identical), and a statue is genidentical to the particular piece of marble from which it was made (although again, both are not identical).

Timeout: Genidentity is a concept rarely used in operations management. But ask yourself—do you have an identity? You as a kid, or even you 1 minute ago, are not, strictly speaking, identical to yourself now (simply because you are older, taller, maybe smarter—so your former self and your current self do not have all the same properties in common). Rather, what you have is a genidentity. The identity concept neglects that all objects are just a snapshot of their process of existence. It neglects that "real" objects continuously change. The identity concept does not work for real life—but the genidentity concept does. This is why we introduce it here.

On the one hand, it is not correct to say Patient A before a medical operation is identical to Patient A after a medical operation. Similarly, we cannot say that a product is identical to itself while being transformed in a production process. On the other hand, in practice we use ID tags and order numbers to identify products and patients as being this product/patient and no other. To bridge the gap between the correct use of concepts and what we do in practice, we therefore extend the identity concept by referring to genidentity.

Now that we have clarified our (gen)identity concept, we can define the customer penetration and inventory/order separation point. Let's start with the customer penetration point.

Customer Penetration Point

This is the point where an order is created from the customer's perspective, e.g. a transformed resource is bound to a specific customer or customer group. This is illustrated in Figure 4.6. The product/service receives a "stamp" or genidentity that marks it out as belonging to a particular customer or customer group.

Customization (Qualitative)

The "stamp," "mark," or genidentity is based on a qualitative product/service property.

Customization (Quantitative)

The "stamp," "mark," or genidentity is based on physical features (bells and whistles).

An example for *qualitative* customization is that the customer orders a pizza with the dough made by Anthony. An example for *quantitative*

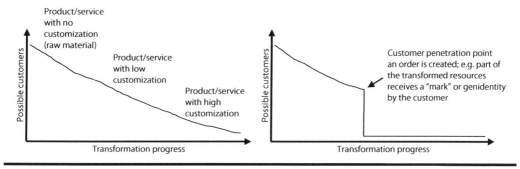

Figure 4.6   Illustration of the customer penetration point.

customization is that the customer wants a pizza from low-gluten flour or a pizza with 100 different kinds of cheese. In both cases, the pizza is bound to a customer/customer group by this customization.

In order for a company to realize this customization, i.e. for the company to ensure that the customer receives a pizza with the dough made by Anthony and/or low-gluten flour, the production control system has to uniquely identify the pizza. The point where the transformed resource is uniquely identified by the production control system is referred to as the inventory/order separation point.

Inventory/Order Separation Point

This is the point where an order is created from the production control system's point of view, e.g. a transformed resource is uniquely identified by the production control system, such as by a specific order number, ID tag, etc. This is where the transformed resource receives a stamp, mark, or genidentity from the production control system.

Inventory Control Problem

The production control system does not uniquely identify a transformed resource. Rather, it controls the inventory levels of a certain group of parts or products, where each individual product is interchangeable.

Order Control Problem

The production control system uniquely identifies a transformed resource. It controls the flow of uniquely identifiable orders through the shop floor.

In an inventory control problem, production control would seek to stabilize the level of inventory between each station. Let's look at an example. Our pizza place has three stations—dough, cheese, and the oven. As soon as a customer comes in and places an order, the oven bakes an assembled pizza and gives it to the customer (assembled to stock but cooked to order). The cheese and dough stations then replenish the inventory. This is only possible if pizzas are standard. If the customer would like a pizza with the dough made by Anthony (and it is normally made by Francesco), the customer would not be happy. To make the customer happy, the pizza place has to tell Anthony to make the dough and to control the flow of this specific pizza. This is an order control problem. In other words, to accommodate the customer penetration point (a pizza with dough made by Anthony), the company has to create an inventory/order separation point (to control the flow of this specific pizza with the dough made by Anthony).

The literature often does not differentiate between these two points and uses them interchangeably. However, this neglects the fact that although the customer penetration point is dictated by the customer, the inventory/order separation point is the company's choice (it is defined from the perspective of production control). Companies should situate the inventory/order separation point at the customer penetration point; but in reality this may often not be the case.

Timeout: The previous example illustrates an important aspect. Both the inventory and order control problem may occur in a make-to-order system. One can produce a standard, interchangeable pizza on a make-to-order basis (inventory control problem) and a highly customized pizza that requires unique operations on a make-to-order basis (order control problem). So to-stock/to-order is independent from the customer penetration and inventory/order separation points. To-stock/to-order refers to when the demand occurs. The customer penetration point refers to the degree of customization of this demand (customer genidentity). The inventory/order separation point refers to whether transforming resources are identified by the production control system (control system genidentity). This identification is required to ensure that the customer receives his/her product. So the two points—customer penetration and inventory/order separation—should overlap.

In an inventory control problem, operations can be treated as independent from each other since transformed resources are interchangeable; but in an order control problem, we have dependent events. Therefore, the same control solution cannot be applied. In general,

- In an inventory control problem, you can control each station individually. This allows for direct control.
- In an order control problem, you have to control the mix of orders (dependent operations) on the shop floor in such a way that it results in controlled stations. So control is indirect.

Timeout: The order control problem is more complex than the inventory control problem. So, companies often try to move the customer penetration point "downstream" of a process, e.g. by postponement. This then allows for also shifting the inventory/order penetration point, which reduces the scope of the order control problem to fewer operations.

Finally, both control problems have to be separated by decoupling inventory.

Decoupling Inventory

Inventory that is used to separate or decouple two or more processes is called decoupling inventory. This kind of inventory is not bound to a specific customer. For example, an inventory control problem can be understood as a series of operations decoupled by decoupling inventory. An internal supply chain can be understood as different processes (and related control problems) that are decoupled by parts. An external supply chain can be understood as different processes that are decoupled by supply. Decoupling inventory can be used to decouple different control problems. Decoupling means that fluctuations in one process do not directly propagate to the second process but are absorbed or buffered by fluctuations in inventory.

Inventory Decoupling Point

This is the point in the process where decoupling inventory is situated (see Figure 4.7). The inventory/order separation point is an inventory decoupling point.

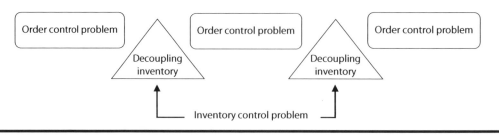

Figure 4.7 Illustration of the inventory decoupling point.

Criterion 3: Routing Characteristics

A process is a series of tasks or operations that bring about a result. These operations typically have to be completed in a certain sequence, i.e. a particular operation must take place before another operation can occur. Each operation (or set of operations) is typically executed at a station. So the sequence of operations in a process dictates the sequence in which stations need to be visited, which is known as the routing.

Routing

The routing of a product/service is the sequence in which stations need to be visited to execute the operations of a process.

Timeout: If there is no constraint on the sequence in which stations have to be visited by a particular order, then the order in essence has no routing. For example, to receive a health certificate you typically need to do a series of health checks, e.g. eyesight, blood test, physical examination, etc. The sequence in which these checks are performed is not typically fixed—you receive the health certificate once all are done. In this book, we assume all orders have a routing. Of course there may be more than one path through the shop, but it should be possible to define a routing or set of alternative routes. If an order has no routing, the control solution can be chosen with disregard for this particular criterion.

The routing is important, since it determines:

■ Where a transformed resource enters and leaves the shop floor
■ Which stations need to be visited
■ The sequence in which the stations must be visited

Card-based systems require feedback on the output rate of transforming resources to control the input rate. Therefore, feedback loops should be established that allow the moment when a transformed resource leaves a station (or the shop floor) to be captured. The feedback loops should feed back this information to the point where new work is waiting to enter the station (or the shop floor). Consequently, the routing has a major influence on from where to where feedback loops need to be established.

Table 4.1   Four Different Types of Shop Floors According to Routing Characteristics

		Number of Operations in the Routing	
		Variable	**Constant**
Flow direction	**Undirected**	Pure job shop	Restricted job shop
	Directed	General flow shop	Pure flow shop

The mix of orders that flow through the shop floor creates different routing characteristics. Routing characteristics can be split into two dimensions:

1. The number of operations in the routing of orders, i.e. whether all orders have the same number of operations (constant routing length) or there are differences between orders (variable routing length)
2. The direction of the sequence, i.e. whether there are fixed upstream and downstream stations (directed routing) or not (undirected routing)

These two dimensions result in four different types of shop floor (see Table 4.1). Based on previous literature, and specifically Oosterman et al. (2000), these four types are named the pure job shop, restricted job shop, pure flow shop, and general flow shop.

There is no difference between a pure job shop and a restricted job shop if we look at the routing probability for each routing step (i.e. the probability that one job moves from one station to the next). So we will only

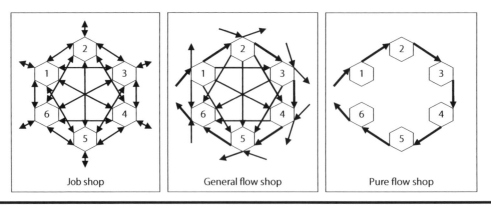

Job shop   General flow shop   Pure flow shop

Figure 4.8   Illustration of the three key types of shop floors according to routing characteristics (the probability of transition between operations is indicated by the strength of the arrows).

talk about job shop routings in general in the rest of this book. The routing characteristics of the pure job shop, restricted job shop, and general flow shop are illustrated in Figure 4.8. The probability of a job transitioning from one station to another is indicated by the thickness of each arrow.

The routing characteristic is a characteristic of the mix of processes that are required to create each product/service flowing through the shop floor. This is different from the layout, which is a property of the shop floor.

Layout

The allocation of stations on the shop floor. In other words, how stations are actually physically positioned on the shop floor.

It is extremely important to note that it is the *routing characteristic* and *not the layout* that helps to determine the applicability of the card-based systems. There often exists confusion, because the layout may reflect the routing characteristic. For example, if many orders have the same routing then transportation distance can be minimized by putting stations (layout) into the sequence based on the typical routing steps. But whether or not stations are organized to reduce transportation waste does not influence the control problem.

If orders have very different routings, the routing cannot be reflected in the layout anyway—there are too many possible routing permutations. In such a case, stations are typically grouped together according to their function or interchangeability, e.g. mills together, lathes together, etc.

The different routing characteristics can occur in any layout as long as the routing is not artificially fixed, e.g. by a conveyor belt. But they typically don't—because trying to realize a pure flow shop in a job shop layout would imply extreme transportation waste. For a true job shop, transportation waste is the same whether there is a job shop layout or a line layout—but capacities can be adjusted, and synergy effects may occur if the same transforming resources are grouped together.

Timeout: Figure 4.9 shows the famous product/process matrix devised by Hayes and Wheelwright (1979). It illustrates a strong correlation observed in practice between the layout type and the volume/degree of customization of the products or services produced by a shop. This matrix arguably reflects the tendency of a firm to minimize transportation waste. But it

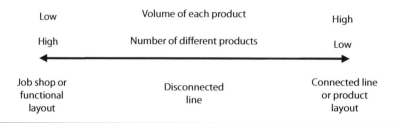

Figure 4.9 Product-process matrix. (Based on Hayes, R. H. and Wheelwright, S. C., *Harvard Business Review*, March–April, 127–136, 1979.)

does not determine the control problem, which is determined by the routing characteristic.

Criterion 4: Variability and Uncertainty in Resource Requirements

The final criterion—variability and uncertainty in resource requirements—has the following two aspects, both illustrated in Figure 4.10:

1. Variability and uncertainty in terms of the processing times of orders
2. Variability and uncertainty in terms of when demand occurs (inter-arrival time)

Timeout: Let's look at our pizza place. The manager knows that at 20:00 there are, on average, 50% more customers than at any other time—so there is variability in demand (although in fact, if this variability occurs always at the same time, it is also called seasonality). But this is just an average value.

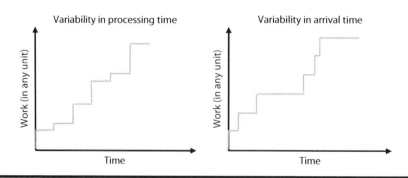

Figure 4.10 Demand curve for illustrating variability in the processing time and variability in the arrival time.

In fact one day is it more than 50%, and another day it is less. This unknown component is the uncertainty in the arrival of demand. Putting cheese on the pizza takes 1 minute for mozzarella and 2 minutes for gorgonzola. So there is variability in processing times too. But again, this is just an average value. Mozzarella may sometimes take 55 seconds and another time take 1 minute and 10 seconds. This is the uncertainty in processing times. Both factors contribute to the variability in resource requirements.

In fact, all four card-based control systems discussed in this book protect the shop floor against variability and uncertainty in the occurrence of demand by withholding work from the shop floor (i.e. by creating a pool of work). So this is no criterion for the application of a certain card-based control system. But an important criterion for the application of card-based systems is variability in processing times.

> *When there is high variability in processing times, some kind of workload balancing (also known as* heijunka*) is required from the card-based control system.*

Workload Balancing (Heijunka)

This refers to creating a mix of work on the shop floor that results in stable stations (i.e. the input of work to a station, measured in processing time, is equal to the output of work). Where there is high variability, a balanced workload will not just happen—the release of work to the shop floor needs to be managed in such a way that the loads across stations are smoothed.

Variability and uncertainty in processing times is (at least partly) in the hands of the company. In fact, reducing unnecessary motion waste, akin to set-up times, is a prerequisite for the implementation of any card-based control system. The existence of large set-up times prohibits the implementation of card-based systems. Thus, where they are present, set-up times need to be reduced before a card-based system can be implemented. This highlights the importance of applying improvement initiatives like the single-minute-exchange-of-die (SMED) approach prior to implementing any control solution.

Timeout: Set-up considerations typically require long or at least mid-term planning. Card-based systems neglect set-up considerations (e.g. if set-up times are sequence dependent) and will likely lead to an increase in set-up times compared to planning and batching. If this increase outweighs the gains obtained from a reduction in inventory, waiting, and overproduction waste, then a card-based system should not be applied. Rather, set-up times need to be reduced first—then and only then can a card-based system be implemented.

Summary: Diagnosing the Control Problem

If you could not follow or remember all of the above—no problem, we will constantly refer back to each criterion when discussing the card-based control systems. So far, it is important to note that:

- The to-stock/to-order interface does not directly influence the choice of control solution. It depends on when demand occurs. To-stock means demand is anticipated. To-order means demand precedes the production/service process. The advantage of to-stock is that the customer does not need to wait. However, two estimation errors are introduced since demand has to be forecasted before the input of work for production is back-scheduled. Meanwhile, there are no estimation errors in a to-order system since operations can be based on actual customer demand. However, the customer has to wait. So the to-stock/to-order interface determines the waste allowance under which the control system operates. Another important difference between to-stock and to-order is that a to-stock system typically has inventory and overproduction waste, while a to-order system has waiting waste since it needs capacity to be available in order to be responsive to customer demand.
- The customer penetration point is where the transformed resources become bound to the customer. The inventory/order separation point is where transformed resources are identified by the production control system. Once a transformed resource is bound to the customer, its flow should be controlled. To achieve this, the production control system has to be able to uniquely identify it. Therefore, the customer penetration and inventory/order separation points should overlap. An inventory control problem is very different from an order control problem. In an inventory control problem, each station is decoupled by decoupling inventory (i.e. inventory that is interchangeable). This allows for controlling each station individually. In an order control problem, the mix of orders on the shop floor needs to be controlled to realize stable stations.

Table 4.2 Summary of Different Criteria for Diagnosing the Control Problem

Criterion	Description	Related Card-Based Control System			
		Kanban/Routing	*ConWIP*	*POLCA/ Routing*	*COBACABANA*
MTS/MTO interface	Does demand occur before transformation or is it anticipated?	Independent (i.e. no influence on the control solution)			
Customer penetration point (inventory/order separation point)	Determined by genidentity; i.e. a transformed resource is bound to the customer; determines the inventory/order separation point (i.e. where in the process a transformed resource is identified by the production control system).	Inventory control problem	Order control problem (all three *kanban*, ConWIP, and COBACBANA are designed for this kind of problem)		
Routing	The sequence in which stations need to be visited.	All routing characteristics (low variability)	Pure flow shop	Only directed routing	All routing characteristics
Processing time variability	Variability and/or uncertainty in processing times.	Low	Low	Low	High
Where discussed?		Chapter 5	Chapter 6	Chapter 7	Chapter 8

- The routing is the sequence in which stations need to be visited to complete the process of operations required for a product/service. It determines (i) where work enters and leaves the process; and (ii) which stations are visited (and in what sequence). It therefore has a major influence on the required structure of feedback loops, which should span from where work leaves to where work enters the system to align the input rate with the output rate.
- Variability in processing times requires a certain degree of workload balancing capabilities. Only by balancing the workload across resources and over time, thus reducing variability, can inventory, overproduction (buffer), and waiting (buffer) waste be reduced.

The four criteria and related card-based control systems are summarized in Table 4.2. Having now identified the criteria against which we can compare and contrast the four different card-based control systems, we can now turn our attention to discussing each of these systems. This is no small task and will take the rest of this book.

Highlights Revisited

- *We outline the difference between to-stock and to-order (the to-stock/to-order interface).* To-stock means that the transforming operations are anticipated and precede the resource requirements. To-order means that the transforming operations only take place once the resource requirements are known. This criterion does not directly affect the applicability of card-based systems but it determines the waste allowance in which they can operate. In a to-stock system, the customer expects zero delivery time. In a to-order system, there always has to be a delivery time allowance. Another important distinction is that to-stock systems mainly suffer from inventory and overproduction waste, while to-order systems suffer from waiting waste.
- *We outline the difference between customer penetration point and inventory/order separation point.* The customer penetration point is the point in the process where the transformed resource (the future product/service) receives a "stamp" or genidentity that marks it out as belonging to a particular customer or customer group. The inventory/order separation point is the point in the process where the transformed resource receives a "stamp" or genidentity from the production control system.

While the customer penetration point is dictated by the customer, the inventory/order separation point is your choice, i.e. it is in the hands of the company. Typically at least, the inventory/order separation point should be located at the customer penetration point. The inventory/order separation point creates two very different control problems: the inventory control problem, where operations can be treated as independent; and the order control problem, where operations are dependent since transformed resources have a genidentity.

■ *We outline the difference between routing and layout.* The routing is a characteristic of the product/service and gives the sequence in which stations must be visited to realize the operations of the process (to create the product/service). The layout is the actual pattern of stations on the shop floor. The routing is a major determinant of the applicability of card-based systems since it determines where work enters and leaves the system—and thus where the feedback loop from the output back to the input needs to be provided.

■ *We discuss the different forms of variability in customer demand.* Customer demand may be variable and uncertain in terms of when it occurs and the processing times involved. Variability in processing times requires some form of workload balancing (also known as *heijunka*) from the card-based control system.

Chapter 5

The Inventory Control Problem: *Kanban* Systems

Highlights

- ■ *We outline the six rules of* kanban *systems.*
- ■ *We outline the difference between a work-in-process* kanban *system and a production* kanban *system.*
- ■ *We outline the implications for the use of* kanban *to control the flow of independent product/service flows through a set of resources (i.e. shop floor control).*
- ■ *We discuss the applicability of* kanban *systems.*

The previous four chapters outlined how we conceptualize a production/service system, what a card-based system is, and what all card-based systems discussed in this book have in common. We also outlined four criteria that determine different control problems. This and the following chapters will now discuss each of the card-based control solutions in the light of these criteria—each suitable for a different control problem. We will start in this chapter with *kanban* systems.

Kanban

A visual signal, *kanban* literally means to watch over a board for a period; it is like a sign outside a business, but with a soul (Protzman et al. 2010). It is typically a sheet of paper/plastic/metal—a physical card (see Figure 5.1 for some

Figure 5.1   Examples of *kanban* cards.

examples). This is why the *kanban* system is called a card-based system—in fact, it is the original card-based system. The card may be integrated into a container or material handling device. Still, this container should also be imagined as a container with a *kanban* attached to it and not as a *kanban* container.

Kanban *System*

We have the *kanbans*, which are card signals; and we also have a *kanban* system, which represents the system created out of the circulating *kanbans*. *Kanbans* can be of different types according to their function—we will get to know withdrawal *kanbans*, work-in-process *kanbans*, production *kanbans*, and common *kanbans*.

We will not discuss all the different *kanban* types that can be found in the literature; there are vendor *kanbans*, inventory *kanbans*, supplier *kanbans*, signal *kanbans*, electronic *kanbans*, etc. Rather, our objective is to reveal the mechanics underlying *kanban* systems. We therefore focus on the types and names that are encountered in the key books from which we derived our insights—particularly Monden (1983), Ohno (1988), and Shingo (1989). This book is not about the names of *kanban* systems, but about how a *kanban* system works, whatever it is called and wherever it operates!

Kanban systems are probably the most widely applied and most highly cited form of card-based system. Yet even this form of card-based system is not really that well understood. A first important aspect often overlooked is that *kanban* systems were developed to connect different product/service flows to one another, as illustrated in Figure 5.2. They were not originally developed to coordinate different product/service flows through the same set of transforming

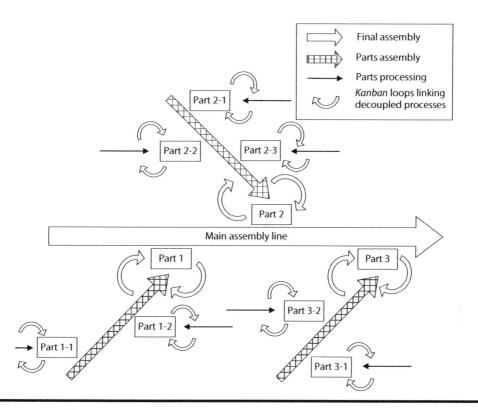

Figure 5.2 *Kanban* **was originally developed to control the internal supply chain—linking processes together.**

resources (where the products/services have to compete for these resources). So, we first have to look at how *kanban* systems were used to control the internal supply chain of a company (the original intention behind *kanban* systems) before we can look at the implications for shop floor control.

Internal Supply Chain

A supply chain coordinates different flows of transformed resources, with one flow joining another like a river; for example, parts flow into subassemblies and subassemblies into assemblies. The flows belong to the company and are thus internal to the company—this can be referred to as an internal supply chain.

Shop Floor Control

The coordination of different product/service flows (transformed resources) through one shop floor (transforming resources). Product/service flows do not converge but remain separated.

Kanban for the Internal Supply Chain: The Six Rules of *Kanban* Systems

The *kanban* system can best be understood by analyzing the six rules of *kanban* systems originally presented by Taiichi Ohno—the inventor of the system. Let's start with the first rule of *kanban* systems. This rule was stated by Ohno (1988, p. 30) as *"The later process goes to the earlier process to pick up products."* We see that this is inconsistent with our definition of a process, which is what the product experiences. Rather, we should refer to the shop floor where the later/earlier process is executed. Since this is quite a cumbersome expression, we use the term "line" instead. In acknowledgment that one process (e.g. a subassembly process) has to precede another process (e.g. the final assembly process), we will call the latter the "main line" and the former the "secondary line." This adjustment has been made throughout the book.

Timeout: We chose the term "line" rather than shop floor since the working of kanbans *is easier to illustrate using lines. The term may have connotations with being straight, inflexible, and standardized. But, of course, a line can also be substituted for a shop floor with a job shop layout. The* kanban *system just controls the input to each line. The* kanban *system in the internal supply chain is used to coordinate the flow of materials at the points where the different lines converge. It is irrelevant to the* kanban *system exactly how each line produces the output (i.e. what happens within the line).*

So the first rule of *kanban* systems is as follows:

First Kanban *Rule*

The later process (*i.e. later, downstream, or main line*) goes to the earlier process (*i.e. earlier, upstream, or secondary line*) to pick up products.

Taiichi Ohno stated that he derived this idea from his visit to an American supermarket back in 1956:

> From the supermarket we got the idea of viewing the earlier process in a production line as a kind of store. The later process (customer) goes to the earlier process (supermarket) to acquire the required parts (commodities) at the time and in the quantity

needed. The earlier process immediately produces the quantity just taken (restocking the shelves). (Ohno 1988, p. 26)

Timeout: The idea that the customer goes to the earlier process underpins any market (not only a supermarket). The contrast can best be understood by comparing a system based on the traveling salesman, where the salesman (earlier process) would go from customer to customer (later process)—as was the system prevalent in Japan in the 1950s—with a system where a market exists, where the customer may go from salesperson to salesperson. In fact, these are the two systems Ohno compares. So it is not the idea of the American supermarket but the idea of the market itself vs. the traveling salesman that is really important.

There are some important observations to be made concerning Ohno's (1988) quote. First, he talked about linking processes. Second, these processes were decoupled by inventory—in the store. As discussed in Chapter 4, decoupling means that fluctuations in one process do not propagate to the second process. Rather, they are absorbed or accommodated by fluctuations in the inventory level. Third, just the quantity taken is replenished—this is the key to avoiding overproduction waste, which was the main concern of Taiichi Ohno. This leads to the second rule of *kanban* systems (Ohno 1988, p. 36).

Second Kanban *Rule*

The earlier process (*i.e. the secondary line*) only produces the amount withdrawn by the later process (*i.e. the main line*).

It is important to note that, if there is variability in the work that is withdrawn by the main line, the secondary line should have capacity to accommodate this variability. This is because, if it is not able to provide the required product on time, the station where the later process is executed may starve—and inventory waste will accumulate in the process. This is why workload balancing (*heijunka*) is so important. It is the only way to avoid the trade-off between large levels of waiting waste in earlier lines and inventory/waiting waste in later lines.

Rule 1 and Rule 2 establish the feedback loop and realize input/output control. The third and the fourth rules of *kanban* systems (Ohno 1988, pp. 40–41) link the flow of transformed resources to *kanban* cards. This establishes the actual *card-based* control system.

Third Kanban *Rule*

Picking up or producing goods without a *kanban* is prohibited.

Fourth Kanban *Rule*

A *kanban* card must be attached to all goods.

The third rule appears to somewhat overlap with the fourth rule of *kanban* systems. But the fourth rule ensures that a *kanban* cannot be used twice. Rule 3 and Rule 4 in fact complement each other. Only when a part is used by the main line does a *kanban* become free and available to use for a different transformed resource. The fourth rule is the key rule to avoiding overproduction. It means that one cannot use a *kanban* to withdraw a part, then just detach the *kanban* from the part before going back and taking another part with the same *kanban*.

But, let's look at how this works. We have a later line, which needs a part; and an earlier line, which produces the parts. Both are linked by a supermarket, store, or inventory decoupling point. All parts in the inventory decoupling point have a so-called work-in-process *kanban* attached to them. Meanwhile, the later or main line uses a so-called withdrawal *kanban* to take material from the supermarket. Hence, we actually have two feedback loops, as illustrated in Figure 5.3.

- A withdrawal *kanban* loop from the later line to the supermarket.
- A work-in-process *kanban* loop from the supermarket to the beginning of the earlier or secondary line.

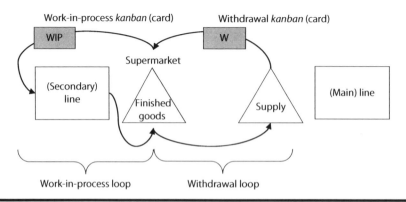

Figure 5.3 Information loops established by work-in-process *kanbans* and withdrawal *kanbans*.

Timeout: Note that loops are established between physical objects (stations) and inventory decoupling points (supermarket). We can't link operations or processes by kanbans *(which are actions). This is why it is so important to differentiate between processes/operations, which are product/service characteristics, and shop floor/stations, which are physical entities where the former take place.*

From Figure 5.3, it appears that the two loops could be independent—but in fact they aren't. They are actually coupled, since withdrawal *kanbans* and work-in-process *kanbans* have to be matched at the supermarket. So, let's work through it step by step.

When the assembly arrives at the main line—this is at the station where the operation that links the later and earlier processes is executed—a subassembly or part is assembled into the assembly. This means that the *kanban* of the part is freed (remember that all transformed resources must have a *kanban* attached to it—Rule 4). This *kanban* becomes the withdrawal *kanban* for a new part. The later process takes the withdrawal *kanban* and goes to the inventory decoupling point (supermarket). This is illustrated in Figure 5.4.

To know which part to withdraw from the supermarket, exactly what the parts are should be written on them. This is one function of the so-called

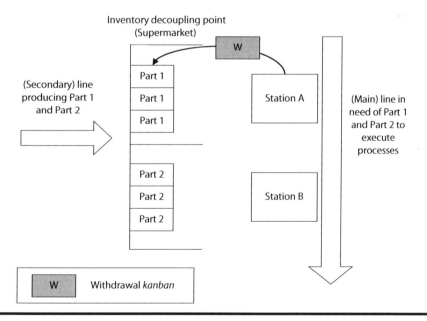

Figure 5.4   Withdrawal *kanban* moves to the inventory decoupling point (supermarket).

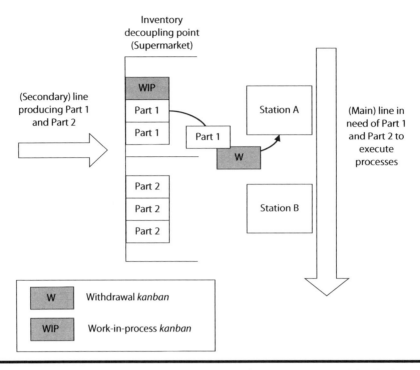

Figure 5.5 Work-in-process *kanban* is detached from the part and both the part and the withdrawal *kanban* move to the main line.

work-in-process *kanban* that is attached to each part in the supermarket. Like in the real supermarket—one not only needs the shopping list (the withdrawal *kanban*) but should also be clear on exactly what each product on the shelf is.

A part with a work-in-process *kanban* matching the withdrawal *kanban* is withdrawn. The work-in-process *kanban* is then detached from the part; and the withdrawal *kanban* and part move together to the main line, as illustrated in Figure 5.5. This closes the withdrawal *kanban* loop.

Timeout: We say that a part is withdrawn. But, in fact, many times we talk about several parts. When this is the case, a fixed device is often used to control the number of parts. This is typically called a kanban *container. As we said before, a* kanban *container should be understood as a container with a* kanban. *Whether the* kanban *system controls a single part or controls a container of parts does not influence how it works—and the main objective of this book is revealing how it works.*

The work-in-process *kanban*, which was freed up in the previous step, now signals to the secondary line that a new part has to be produced, as

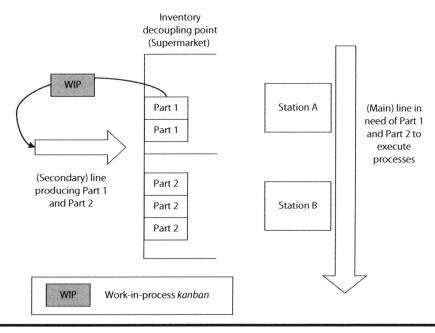

Figure 5.6 Work-in-process *kanban* moves to the beginning of the secondary line (triggering production).

illustrated in Figure 5.6. This signaling to start production is a second function of the work-in-process *kanban*. The part is then produced, which closes the work-in-process loop.

Since there is no good that is produced without a *kanban* (Rule 3), the number of *kanbans* represents an upper limit or WIP-Cap on the work on the shop floor; but only if there is no work without a *kanban* (Rule 4). We saw that if the work-in-process *kanban* is detached from the good in the supermarket, a withdrawal *kanban* has to be attached to it instead. Similarly, after the production of a new part is triggered by the work-in-process *kanban*, the *kanban* (card) has to be attached to the part.

Timeout: "Kanban" here refers to a withdrawal kanban *(for picking up items), or to a work-in-process* kanban, *or to any other type of* kanban. *It has to be understood as a signal of need. In other words, it is prohibited to pick up or produce goods without a need. Goods are pulled through the system based on demand.*

The fifth rule of *kanban* systems refers to defects. In fact, a defect causes major trouble in a *kanban* system, since a *kanban* is attached to the defective part. So the *kanban* of the defective part needs to be eliminated and another *kanban* (sometimes called an emergency *kanban*) must be added at another location in the system. This is extremely cumbersome if there are many loops in the *kanban* system.

Fifth Kanban *Rule*

Products have to be 100% defect free.

We learned before that quality is beyond the realms of a card-based control system. Rule 5 is extremely important for a *kanban* system to work; however, it does not affect the underlying mechanics of the system. So we feel Rule 5 is of a different nature to rules 1 through 4.

Rules 1 through 4 realize the first of the two main principles that actually underpin all four card-based systems, not just *kanban*: to stabilize the quantity of work that flows through the shop floor by input/output control. The second principle, to reduce the quantity of work that flows through the shop floor (the work-in-process), is realized by the sixth rule of *kanban* systems.

Sixth Kanban *Rule*

The number of *kanbans* should be reduced.

For example, Harada (2015) reports that Taiichi Ohno set a goal to limit the work-in-process inventory to five pieces (pp. 60–61). The link between *kanban* cards and work-in-process, which is required to interpret Rule 6 as being about work-in-process reduction, is established by Rule 3 and Rule 4.

Work-in-Process *Kanban* vs. Production *Kanban*

The system described in the previous sections raises an interesting question: How can the withdrawal *kanban* match up to the work-in-process *kanban*? Or, phrased differently, if the withdrawal *kanban* signals that a good is needed (since a good was used), how can the good already be there when the withdrawal *kanban* arrives? The answer is twofold:

- In reality, there always has to be some inventory in the system.

■ The system only works if the withdrawal *kanban* withdraws Part A but not a specific Part A (i.e. individual parts have no genidentity for the production control system).

This means that the system described above only applies to an inventory control problem where the supermarket functions as decoupling inventory. The *kanban* system is therefore some kind of re-order point system driven by *kanbans*. The work-in-process *kanban* signals Part A was used and that more of Part A is needed—not that a specific Part A is needed. In fact, it is based on our interpretation of Shingo (1989), who starts his introduction to *kanban* with the calculation of the re-order point.

Timeout: As an example, let's go back to pizza. You go to the cashier and buy a piece of pepperoni pizza. The receipt is your withdrawal kanban. *You then go to the counter and withdraw the pizza. The clerk selling you the pizza writes on a piece of paper that more pepperoni pizza is needed (the work-in-process* kanban*) and sends this to the start of the pizza making process, which then signals that more pepperoni pizza should be made. For the work-in-process* kanban *system to work, it is clear that*

1. *There must always be some inventory of pepperoni pizza, as otherwise you get hungry.*
2. *At that moment, you can only withdraw the pepperoni pizza that is physically there. If you want a pizza with vegetarian pepperoni, you have to wait (getting hungry again).*

But how does the point that a work-in-process *kanban* system always has to have inventory in the supermarket fit with Ohno's (1988) objective of avoiding inventory and overproduction? Well, it doesn't! In fact, Ohno (1988) and Shingo (1989) describe two different *kanban* systems. We assume both were applied somewhere in Toyota, yet the two are inherently different.

Timeout: We see production control at Toyota as a network of different kanban *systems—one system nested inside the other. This nesting of different* kanban *systems is an important aspect. It is valid for all card-based control systems described in this book; and this is something we will come back to later in Chapter 10. It is more than valid to nest one card-based system into another, whether this is two types of* kanban *or aspects of two completely different card-based systems. While it may be sometimes implied in the*

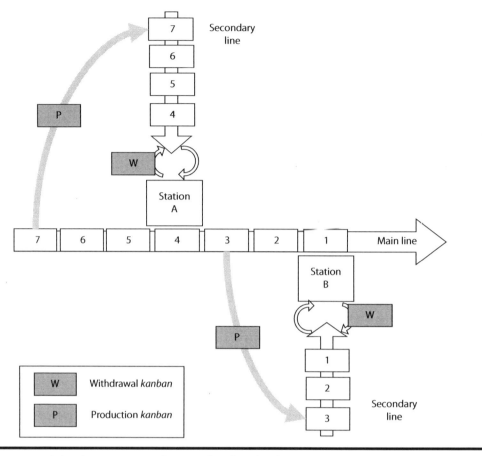

Figure 5.7   A *kanban* system using production *kanbans*.

literature that these systems are mutually exclusive—there are, in fact, no purity concerns in the sense that there is no need to apply one and only one card-based system.

Ohno (1988) uses a production *kanban* instead of the work-in-process *kanban* mentioned in Shingo (1989). This production *kanban* is sent to the secondary line before the product that requires the part arrives at the station on the main line where the part is used. A production *kanban* system is illustrated in Figure 5.7.

This change has two main consequences:

■ The decoupling inventory at the supermarket is not necessarily required anymore—zero overproduction/inventory is theoretically possible. We say "theoretically" since inventory often will still be used to protect the system; but it is not a must as in the work-in-process *kanban* system.

■ The production *kanban* and the transformed resource related to it (produced on the secondary line) can be bound to one specific transformed resource on the main line (identified by the withdrawal *kanban*). Individual parts can have a genidentity for the production control system, which allows for customized parts.

Timeout: In a work-in-process kanban *system, you may go to a bakery and buy some of the bread that is in stock there. The baker then replenishes the bread. In a production* kanban *system, you call the baker 60 minutes before you go to the bakery (which is 60 minutes away from you) and tell him which bread you want (you send him the production* kanban*). The baker then makes your bread so it is ready in 60 minutes when you arrive to pick it up (fresh and hot from the oven).*

The literature often criticizes kanban *for not being able to accommodate customized products (e.g. Hopp and Spearman 2001; Suri 2010). It is often argued that this would result in large levels of inventory since, for each different part, inventory should be on-hand. But we have seen that this criticism only holds for a work-in-process* kanban *system, which is in fact a re-order point system based on* kanban *signals. It is not valid for a system based on production* kanbans*, as described in Ohno (1988)—such a system (theoretically) allows for full customization while having zero inventory.*

We said that the production *kanban* system can "theoretically" realize zero inventory/overproduction. The major restriction is the flow time. For the system to work, the flow time of the product (part) on the secondary line (which carries the production *kanban*) must be equal to or less than the flow time of the product on the main line (which carries the corresponding withdrawal *kanban*). This relationship is illustrated in Figure 5.8. Since the flow time is often dependent on the customization of the product/service, there is a trade-off between customization and the inventory level.

There are two means of synchronizing the flow time on the secondary and main lines so that the part produced on the secondary line arrives at the station where the secondary and main lines converge at the same time as the product from the main line:

■ Workload balancing (*heijunka*)
■ Extra capacity on the secondary line

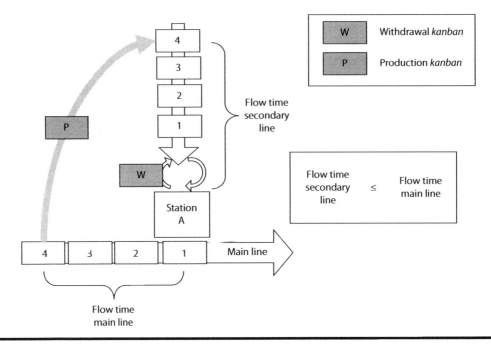

Figure 5.8   The relationship between the flow time on the main and secondary lines.

Timeout: We have referred to workload balancing, or heijunka, *in the previous chapter, but it is extremely important here to understand workload balancing (or* heijunka*) as leveling the load of the main and secondary lines! The mix of goods on the main line should be such that the flow time on the main and secondary lines are equal. Of course, this is rarely the case, and waiting waste is created on the secondary lines—still, this waste should be minimized. Heijunka is therefore not just about leveling the load on the main line. It is about leveling the load in the whole system by controlling the sequence in which products are produced on the main line. Waste is waste on the main and secondary lines—so all lines need to be balanced.*

Heijunka *(Internal Supply Chain)*

Refers to load leveling or balancing. But it is load balancing for the whole *kanban* system, not for one single line. Toyota balanced the main line with all secondary lines in mind. Only this approach was able to ensure the functioning of the Toyota Production System.

Timeout: This understanding of heijunka *questions our interpretation of the* heijunka *box. The* heijunka *box is often considered a device for achieving* heijunka *(e.g. load balancing). However, the* heijunka *box—as illustrated*

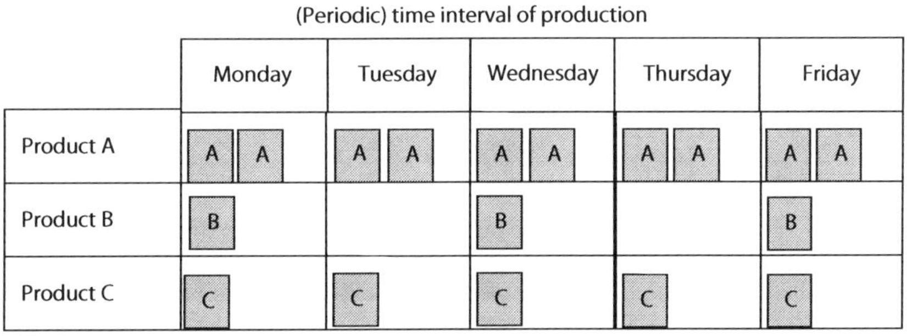

(Periodic) time interval of production

	Monday	Tuesday	Wednesday	Thursday	Friday
Product A	A A	A A	A A	A A	A A
Product B	B		B		B
Product C	C	C	C	C	C

Figure 5.9 *Heijunka* **box storing** *kanbans* **for future entry to the main line.**

in Figure 5.9—is just a visual device to ensure the schedule on the main line. By itself, it does not allow for any load leveling or balancing; in fact, Monden (1983) suggests that the actual load balancing calculations should be executed using a heuristic computer program (p. 60). The heijunka *box is essentially a* kanban *card storage device for orders waiting to be released to the system. It can therefore be considered, except in name, to be a pre-shop pool of orders.*

So there are three different *kanbans*, where each creates a different kind of information loop and serves a different function; see Table 5.1. It is not

Table 5.1   The Three Types of *Kanbans*

Kanban Type	Used Where?	Used For?	Important Remarks
Withdrawal *kanban*	Between the main line and the supermarket (inventory decoupling point).	Ensures that the right good is withdrawn from the supermarket.	May be the work-in-process/production *kanban* of the main line.
Work-in-process *kanban*	Between the supermarket (inventory decoupling point) and the beginning of the secondary line.	Signals to the beginning of the secondary line that a good *was* used.	Is often realized by a so-called *kanban* container. Importantly, the goods to which a *kanban* relates are interchangeable.
Production *kanban*	Between the main line and the beginning of the secondary line.	Signals to the beginning of the secondary line that a good *will be* used.	Contains production information. Is bound to one specific withdrawal *kanban* (and the corresponding transforming resource).

the *kanban* itself (i.e. its physical properties) that determines what type of *kanban* it is, but its function. For example, the work-in-process *kanban* for one line may become the withdrawal *kanban* for an earlier line. Similarly, if the output of the secondary line moves directly to the supply of the main line rather than passing an explicit supermarket, then the withdrawal *kanban* loop and consequently the withdrawal *kanban* is not required.

Another major difference is that work-in-process *kanbans* typically stay within one loop, e.g. if a part is assembled, the same work-in-process *kanban* is used for another part. Meanwhile, production *kanbans* may only be used for one specific product (this is why they are also sometimes called job-order *kanbans*). Since work-in-process *kanbans* can be re-used, they are often realized using so-called *kanban* containers. The *kanban* container is a physical storage device that is linked to a *kanban*. For example, rather than sending a *kanban* card, an empty *kanban* container is sent to signal the start of production.

Timeout: A permanent link between kanban *and container may create some problems. In such a scenario, the container will one time function as a withdrawal* kanban *between the main line and supermarket, and the other time as a work-in-process* kanban *between the supermarket and secondary line. Decoupling container and* kanban *(just attaching* kanbans *to containers) resolves this ambiguity.*

The previous discussion has explored the use of *kanban*s for linking product/service flows, i.e in the context of the environment for which they were originally developed—the internal supply chain. Next, we will explore the implications of using *kanban*s to control the flow of work through one shop floor.

Kanban for Shop Floor Control

The *kanban* system was developed to link different product/service flows together. Meanwhile, in shop floor control we coordinate independent product/service flows through a set of transforming resources. The objective is to coordinate transformed resources and transforming resources on the shop floor.

If we would apply the *kanban* system as it is discussed above, then two stations would be linked as illustrated in Figure 5.10.

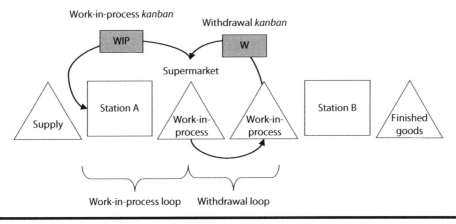

Figure 5.10   The original *kanban* as a shop floor control system.

However, often an explicit work-in-process inventory after Station A (the supermarket) is not required. Rather, products completed at Station A move directly to the queue at Station B. This eliminates the need for a withdrawal *kanban* loop. Instead of two loops and an exchange of *kanban* cards, there is only one loop of either work-in-process or production *kanban* cards from Station B to Station A, telling Station A that a certain product was or will be used. Since it may be both (work-in-process or production *kanban*) it is called a common *kanban*. Hence, all three types of *kanban* in the internal supply chain are substituted for one *kanban* type; see Table 5.2.

Instead of two loops and an exchange of *kanban* cards, there is only one loop of common *kanban* cards from Station B to Station A, telling Station A that a certain product was or will be used. Station A then replenishes the product. This is illustrated in Figure 5.11.

Table 5.2   *Kanban* Types for Process Control

Kanban *Type in the Internal Supply Chain*	*Substituted on the Shop Floor By*	*What Is It Used For?*	*Important Remarks*
Withdrawal *kanban*	Common *kanban*	Ensures that the right good is withdrawn	Can be kept as a separated *kanban*
Work-in-process *kanban*		Signals to the earlier operation that a good *was* used	Creates an inventory control system
Production *kanban*		Signals to the earlier operation that a good *will be* used	Creates an order control system

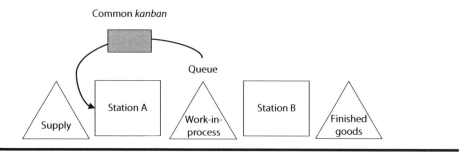

Figure 5.11 ***Kanban*** **as a shop floor control system.**

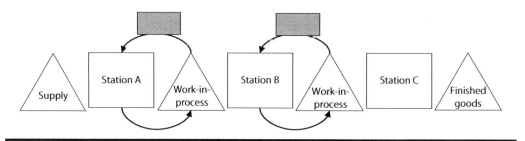

Figure 5.12 **A typical system of *kanban* loops, as often depicted in the literature.**

These single common *kanban* loops between stations then result in the typical loop structure we often encounter in the literature (see Figure 5.12).

In an *inventory control problem*, Station C, for example, takes a product (transformed resource) and tells Station B that the product "was" used. Station B then replenishes the product withdrawn by Station C. It is therefore assumed that the required transformed resource is already waiting for Station C. The level of work-in-process is controlled by limiting the number of *kanban* cards within each loop. When a product enters a loop, a *kanban* card belonging to that loop is attached to it. If it leaves this loop, the *kanban* card is detached and the production of a new product is authorized.

When Station C uses a transformed resource from Station B, Station B replenishes the good. When Station B uses a transformed resource from Station A (for example to replenish the good used by Station C), Station A replenishes the good, and so on. This creates a chain of decoupled loops—as depicted in Figure 5.13—where stations are both using transformed resources and replenishing transformed resources.

In an *order control problem*, Station C has to tell Station A that it needs a certain part (and no other part). The *kanban* signals that a specific product, which is still to be produced, "will be" used at the following station. For example, the customer wants a pizza with the dough made by Anthony.

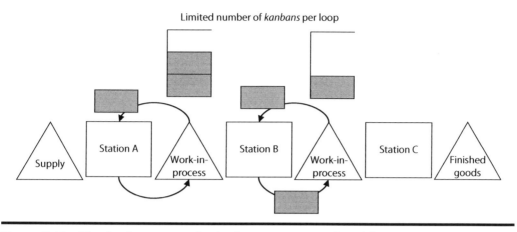

Figure 5.13 The *kanban* system in the inventory control problem.

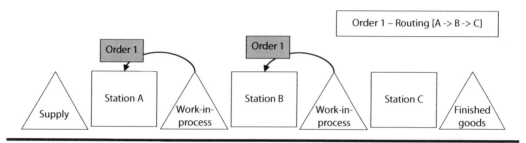

Figure 5.14   In an order control problem, *kanbans* need to be propagated to the station where the order enters the system.

If the dough is done by Station A, then Station C has to tell Station A that, for this pizza, it should be Anthony and not Francesco doing the dough. Thus, Station A sends a specific *kanban* to Station B (saying one pizza with dough by Anthony), Station B then sends a specific *kanban* to Station A, and then Station A starts producing the order. Hence, *kanbans* need to propagate information to the station where the customer penetration point is located. As we saw, this is typically also the inventory/order separation point. This propagation is illustrated in Figure 5.14.

While the order is processed at Station A, the *kanban* from Station C has to wait at Station B until the order arrives from Station A (see Figure 5.15).

So the set of *kanbans* in a loop consist of those *kanbans* that currently belong to direct work (i.e. where the transformed resources to which a *kanban* belongs is already queuing at the station) and those *kanbans* that currently relate to indirect work (i.e. where the transformed resource to which a *kanban* belongs is still upstream at another station). This is illustrated in Figure 5.16.

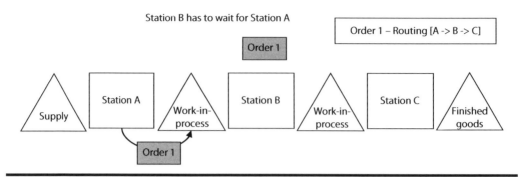

Figure 5.15   In an order control problem, the *kanbans* of downstream stations may have to wait for the associated order to arrive from upstream stations.

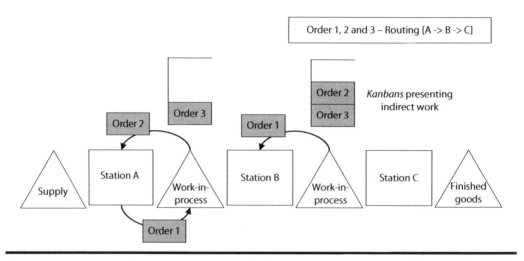

Figure 5.16   In an order control system, *kanbans* may represent direct and indirect work to a station.

Direct Work(load)

The work to be processed at a transforming resource that is currently waiting at this resource.

Indirect Work(load)

The work to be processed at a transforming resource that is currently at a preceding (or upstream) resource.

Timeout: It is important to remember that, in an order control problem, a kanban *belongs to an order—a transformed resource is uniquely identified by the production control system. The* kanban *belongs, for example, to the pizza with the dough made by Anthony. This pizza is still not at the cheese station because Anthony does it (so it represents indirect load to the station). The* kanban *has to wait until the specific pizza arrives. Once the pizza arrives, the (same)* kanban *represents direct load. In other words, a* kanban *represents indirect load if the transformed resource indicated by it has not arrived. It represents direct load if the transformed resource indicated by it has actually arrived at the station.*

So for the system to run, we need to allow for two times as many *kanban* cards at the second station as at the first, three times as many at the third station, four times as many at the fourth station, and so on. In other words, the WIP-Cap applied has to increase the further downstream a station is positioned to allow for the *kanban* cards that must wait for their related order to arrive. This means the last station has the highest WIP-Cap or limit on the number of *kanbans*. Because the *kanban* system is controlled by the last station, it may become impossible to control the system since the last station has to allow too many orders to enter the system.

Timeout: Imagine a line with six stations through which orders flow that have six operations, all with the same routing (a pure flow shop). The shop should have six kanbans *at the last station and one* kanban *at the first station; remember that we have an order control problem—where we have to control the orders and can't just focus on inventory levels. Controlling the system from the last station means you have to control the release of six orders in such a way that there is always work at the first station. Wouldn't it be much easier to just let orders enter at the first station one by one? The problem is not really critical if operations are standardized, since a new job is just released each standardized operation throughput time. But the problem becomes very tricky when there are high levels of customization, and when processing times or even routings vary.*

The important point to remember is that, in an inventory control problem, *kanbans* just represent direct work to a station—each station just replenishes what has been used by the next station (to serve its customer). For example, in our pizza scenario, we could have pre-prepared pizzas at each station (functioning as decoupling inventory). In an order control problem, *kanbans* represent both direct and indirect work. This means that the last station in the process needs to allow for the largest number of *kanbans*—to allow for its own direct load and the indirect load from all of the preceding stations. Imagine—should be easy by now—a pizza process of making dough, putting cheese on, and baking the assembled pizza. Each pizza is individually made for each customer. When customer arrives, the baking station sends a *kanban* to the cheese station for a pizza with cheese. Then the *kanban* card has to wait for the pizza with cheese to arrive. The cheese station sends a *kanban* to the dough station for the pizza dough, then this *kanban* card has to wait for the pizza dough to arrive. To avoid waiting, the baking station should be allowed to have three *kanbans*, the cheese station to have two *kanbans*, and so on. For the baking station, allowing for three *kanbans* means (in the ideal case) that one *kanban* belongs to the pizza currently at the baking station, one to the pizza currently at cheese, and one to the pizza currently at the dough station. This is illustrated in Figure 5.17.

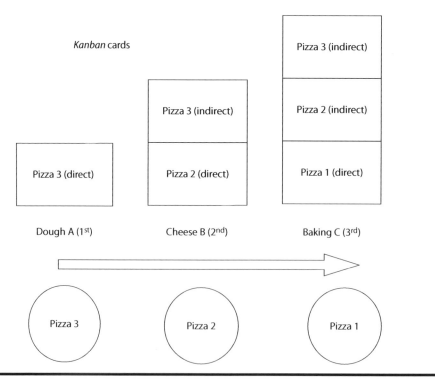

Figure 5.17   Direct vs. indirect load—pizza example.

Applicability of *Kanban* Systems

Kanban systems are highly flexible control solutions. They can be applied to all kinds of control problems. But as they were originally developed for the internal supply chain, it is this environment where they are most effective. Although they can be applied to control the shop floor, there are some important restrictions that we must be aware of.

Let's start with the customer penetration or inventory/order separation point. *Kanban* systems are a powerful solution for an inventory control problem—i.e. where each station is decoupled from all other stations by some form of decoupling inventory. However, using *kanbans* to solve an order control problem raises three issues with the propagation of information to the first station where the order enters the system:

1. How to let common *kanbans,* which are re-used within each loop, represent specific orders rather than more general product types.
2. How to avoid unnecessary starvation caused by a *kanban* that cannot be propagated at a downstream station, even though upstream stations are starving and could start working on the order.
3. How to control the process given that the last station—which is supposed to control the process—requires allowing for the largest number of *kanbans.* In other words, how can a tight (or small) WIP-Cap be realized at an upstream station while allowing the downstream station to have a looser (or larger) WIP-Cap?

Overcoming these issues, and providing a card-based solution for the order control problem, was one of the main motivational factors behind the development of alternative card-based systems to *kanban.*

Another criterion is routing variability. While it is often assumed that *kanbans* can only be applied in a pure flow shop, this is not strictly true. Rather, *kanbans* can easily be used to build overlapping loops across stations to accommodate a certain degree of routing variability. An example of a multiloop *kanban* system is given in Figure 5.18. However, a main limitation of a multiloop *kanban* system is that loops need to be established to reflect the routing steps of all products/services flowing through the shop floor—which can be difficult in high—variety contexts.

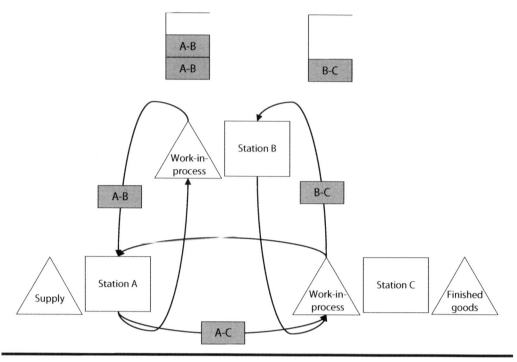

Figure 5.18 A multiloop *kanban* system.

Finally, *kanban* systems do not incorporate any mechanism for achieving load balancing. Rather, they focus on stabilizing the number of products/parts in the system. This means that the workload is only balanced if processing time variability is low. *Kanban* systems should therefore not be applied if the variability in processing times is high. In general, *kanban* systems keep information on work local to a station, which hinders load balancing across stations on the shop floor. We learned above that load balancing or *heijunka* is important for *kanban* systems to work. However, *heijunka* is not realized by the *kanban* system itself—it precedes it.

Summary: *Kanban* Systems

Kanban systems were developed in the 1950s/1960s for controlling the internal supply chain at Toyota, and in more recent decades they have become popular worldwide. They have been used to link together different processes or flows of transformed resources. The latter process has to go to the line where the earlier process was executed to get the required transformed resources. The earlier line produces what was used or what will be used—according to the *kanban* type applied. There is not one universal *kanban* system but several *kanbans* and related functions; for example, we identified withdrawal *kanbans*, work-in-process *kanbans*, and production *kanbans*. These different *kanbans* create two different systems, both potentially incorporating withdrawal *kanbans*:

■ A work-in-process *kanban* system is used to replenish what has been used. It is essentially a re-order point system. It is the kind of system typically considered to be a *"kanban"* in the literature and in practice—as used in repetitive manufacturing.
■ A production *kanban* system synchronizes two lines. The main line signals to a secondary line what it should produce and when—so the part is produced and arrives at the main line at the same time as the corresponding assembly. So it signals what will be used in the future. This system "theoretically" allows inventory to be completely avoided while realizing maximum customization.

While *kanbans* were developed for the internal supply chain, the focus of our book is on what happens within each line or shop floor. Applying the *kanban* system to control independent product/service flows through the shop floor changes the structure of the *kanban* system. Rather than maintaining three *kanbans*, only one *kanban* type is now required. If this common *kanban* signals that a transformed resource "was" used, we have an inventory control problem. Products must therefore be interchangeable so the product used by the later operation is already completed by the preceding station. So we have decoupling inventory between each station.

In an order control problem, only a specific transformed resource can be used—and this information needs to be propagated through the shop floor to get to the station where the first operation in the routing of the order takes place. The common *kanban* signals to each preceding station that there "will be" a specific transformed resource required. The later station then has to wait until all preceding stations have completed the specific order identified by the *kanban*. This propagation process is hindered by:

1. The need to transmit specific information on a *kanban* that is continuously re-used in the loop between two stations.
2. The introduction of starvation or idle resources, since a downstream station may hinder propagation even though an upstream station is starving.

3. The need for a greater number of cards at downstream stations (since a *kanban* is bound to a specific order that still may not have arrived), which runs counter to the idea of controlling the process from the last station (i.e. where the need actually occurs).

These three issues significantly affect the applicability of *kanban* systems to an order control problem.

Meanwhile, *kanban* systems allow for overlapping loops and can accommodate a certain degree of routing variety. But the fact that all routing steps have to be covered by a *kanban* loop prohibits its use in environments with high routing variety. Another issue is that realizing backflows, i.e. allowing for some jobs flowing from Station A to Station B as well as for some jobs flowing from Station B to Station A, is cumbersome. Thus, routings should be directed in a *kanban* system.

Finally, since *kanban* systems do not integrate workload balancing, they are sensitive to variability in processing times.

Highlights Revisited

■ *We outline the six rules of* kanban *systems.* #1 The later process (*i.e. later, downstream, or main line*) goes to the earlier process (*i.e. earlier, upstream, or secondary line*) to pick up products. #2 The earlier process (*i.e. the secondary line*) only produces the amount withdrawn by the later process (*i.e. the main line*). #3 Picking up or producing goods without a *kanban* is prohibited. #4 A *kanban* card must be attached to all goods. #5 Products have to be 100% defect free. #6 The number of *kanbans* should be reduced. Rule 1 and Rule 2 realize the first of the two main principles underlying all four card-based systems: to stabilize the quantity of work that flows through the shop floor by input/output control. Rule 3 and Rule 4 establish *kanban* cards as means of achieving input-output control. The second principle, to reduce the quantity of work that flows through the shop floor (the work-in-process), is realized by the sixth rule of *kanban* systems.

■ *We outline the difference between a work-in-process* kanban *system and a production* kanban *system. Kanban* systems were developed to control the internal supply chain, i.e. the confluence of different product/service flows. A work-in-process *kanban* system is essentially a re-order point system. The later (or main) line goes to the supermarket and withdraws what is needed. The earlier (or secondary) line then replenishes what was used. The supermarket functions as decoupling inventory. Hence, some inventory is in fact required for the system to work. A production *kanban* system synchronizes different lines, which makes decoupling inventory "theoretically" superfluous. In a production *kanban* system, the later (or main) line signals to the earlier line what will be used ahead of the moment when the transformed resource is needed. The transformed resource is then withdrawn from the earlier line when it is needed at the later line.

■ *We outline the implications for the use of* kanban *to control the flow of independent product/service flows through a set of resources (i.e. shop floor control).* In the internal supply chain, two *kanban* loops are used: one between the later (or main) line and the end of the earlier line (or secondary), and one between the end of the earlier (or secondary line) and the beginning of this line. Both are separated by decoupling inventory (the supermarket). However, when we talk about shop floor control, an explicit supermarket is often not required; rather, products flow directly into the queue of the next station. The withdrawal *kanban* loop from this queue to the supermarket is no longer required. Stations are connected by a series of single loops.

■ *We discuss the applicability of* kanban *systems. Kanban* systems are highly effective solutions for the internal supply chain and for shop floor control in the inventory control problem—i.e. when stations are decoupled from each other. However, for an order control problem, *kanban* systems run into several significant problems, such as with propagating information from the last station to the first station. *Kanban* systems also require low routing variability and a directed routing. Finally, since *kanban* systems do not integrate load balancing, processing time variability should be low in order for them to be effective.

Chapter 6

The Low Variability Order Control Problem: ConWIP

Highlights

- *We outline ConWIP and compare it to* kanban *systems.*
- *We discuss the applicability of ConWIP.*

We learned in the previous chapter that the major factor that prohibits the application of *kanban* systems to an order control problem (i.e. where the flow of an order through the shop floor is controlled and operations are dependent) is the propagation of information on which order to release from one station to another. For example, if there is an order requiring stations A, B, and C, then Station C cannot directly signal to Station A. It needs to signal to Station B, which then sends a signal to Station A. The order is then released, but only when it arrives at Station C can station C work on it. In between, the *kanban* cards at Station B and at C have to wait for the transformed resources to arrive—they represent the indirect work to the station rather than the direct work. An easier solution for the propagation of information in the order control problem would be for the last station (Station C) to signal directly to the first station (Station A). This is the solution provided by constant work-in-process (ConWIP).

Constant Work-In-Process (ConWIP)

This system was presented as an alternative card-based control system to *kanban* by Mark L. Spearman, Wallace J. Hopp, and David L. Woodruff (see, e.g. Spearman et al. 1990; Hopp and Spearman 2001). ConWIP uses one feedback loop from the exit to the entry point of a system. This loop is used to circulate cards that represent jobs and, by controlling the number of cards, enforce a maximum limit on the number of jobs in the system. It has been best known for its applications in the semiconductor industry.

But let's first step back and look at the overall differences between ConWIP and *kanban* systems.

ConWIP: How Does It Work?

Let's imagine a job, say Order 1, that has to go from Station A to Station B to Station C. In a *kanban* system, information is propagated from Station A to Station B to Station C, as described in the introduction to this chapter and illustrated in Figure 6.1.

It would be much smarter (and quicker) if Station C were to signal directly to Station A that it should produce Order 1. This is in fact what work-in-process *kanbans* and production *kanbans* do in the internal supply chain—but not on the shop floor. We saw that, in the internal supply chain, these *kanbans* signal from the end of the line to the beginning of the line that a part *was* or *will be* used; and that, consequently, another of that part should be produced. This is illustrated in Figure 6.2.

This is similar to what ConWIP does. The major difference between a *kanban* system and a ConWIP system is that ConWIP cards are

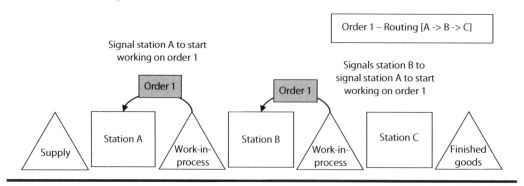

Figure 6.1   Propagation of information to start Order 1 in a *kanban* system.

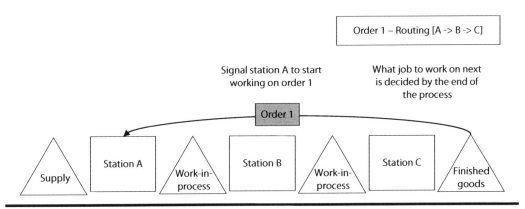

Figure 6.2 Propagation of information to start Order 1 in a system where cards are not anonymous (*kanban* in the internal supply chain).

anonymous—i.e. they don't relate to a specific transformed resource. ConWIP cards signal from the end of the line to the start that *a job* has left the system (as illustrated in Figure 6.3), meaning another one can enter the system (with the card). There is no specification as to which job should enter the shop floor. Cards can also no longer provide information on the work content of a job.

As a result of (job) anonymous cards, the beginning of the process determines which job will enter the system next in a ConWIP system. In contrast, in a *kanban* system, it is the end of the process that determines the job that should be started next. The beginning of the process consequently changes its function when we switch from a *kanban* to a ConWIP system. It is here, at the beginning of the process, that the decision on which job to release next to the system is taken.

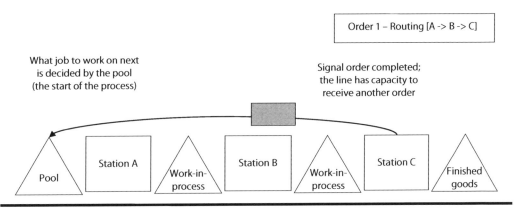

Figure 6.3 Propagation of information to start an Order in a ConWIP system (i.e. anonymous cards).

ConWIP can be described by two simple rules. The first rule of ConWIP is similar to the first rule of *kanban* and ensures that only if there is output should there be input. However, the later line (station) does not tell the earlier line (station) what is needed. Rather, it says that it has capacity to work on a job.

ConWIP Rule 1

The last station signals to the first station in a line that a job was complete.

Meanwhile, the second ConWIP rule ensures the WIP-Cap is enforced. Ensuring that the production control system is effective—i.e. produces what is needed—is the responsibility of the first station in the line. It should start the right job, e.g. in terms of urgency.

ConWIP Rule 2

Whenever the number of jobs in the line is below the pre-established limit, a new job is started by the first station.

Timeout: Much has been written on how ConWIP is better than kanban. *But most of this literature considers* kanban *for shop floor control. This is a general fallacy—although most of the* kanban *literature considers its use for shop floor control, this was not its original intention. We believe that some of the confusion may have arisen out of a misinterpretation of the* kanban *system depicted in Sugimuri et al. (1977, p 561) and Shingo (1989, p 182). Both figures seem to resemble our figure for the use of* kanban *for shop floor control. Importantly, in both figures the authors talk about part processing, part assembly, and final assembly! So both figures (Sugimuri's and Shingo's) present the internal supply chain. If cards were anonymous, then each individual (work-in-process)* kanban *loop depicted by the authors would actually resemble a ConWIP system.*

The Applicability of ConWIP

ConWIP uses a single loop from the end of the line to the start of the line. This is a simple approach for propagating information and provides a straightforward solution for the order control problem. However, it has less potential to control work at each station in an inventory control system compared to a *kanban* system. ConWIP just controls the load in the whole system and disregards the load situation at individual stations.

The applicability of ConWIP also suffers from severe restrictions in terms of routing characteristics:

1. All work has to enter the shop floor at one particular point and leave the shop floor at one particular point so that the number of orders in the system can be controlled by a ConWIP loop.
2. Between entry and exit, all orders must visit the same stations (the flow of orders must not split).
3. The number of stations covered by the ConWIP loop should not be too long.

The first restriction just reflects the fact that there must be two points that establish the loop, and all order routings must be contained by this loop. The second point highlights the fact that work at each station is not controlled; a stable shop floor does not necessarily mean that stations are stable. ConWIP just stabilizes the work on the shop floor (in our case, the line). If there is only one flow, each station works on the same number of jobs, but if the flow of jobs splits then stations on one routing may be overloaded while another is empty. So ConWIP can only be applied in a pure flow shop, i.e. where all orders visit all stations in the same sequence.

Timeout: If orders do not visit all stations in the same sequence, the flow of orders is split. For example, let's assume we have four stations. And let's further assume that we have two types of orders: one order type that visits two stations and another order type that visits the other two stations. Both types of order have the same processing time—so we neglect for the sake of this example the effect of processing time variability, and only focus on the routing. ConWIP only controls the number of orders in the system. It does not consider which stations are actually visited. This means that the line will only be stable if half of the orders in the system are of one type and half the orders are of the other type. Otherwise, the system will be unbalanced, which will lead to overload and starvation (or idleness). Another issue is that the actual work-in-process cap (WIP-Cap) at each station is very different from the one set. For example, if the WIP-Cap is 10 orders, then only in the case of five orders of each type is there a balance. But the actual realized WIP is five not 10 (the theoretical WIP-Cap). Meanwhile, the system could also be made up of 10 jobs of the first type and zero of the second. So now two stations will be starving and two stations will be heavily loaded. Therefore, the use of ConWIP should be restricted to the pure flow shop.

The third point in the list—concerning the number of stations—highlights a linear relationship between the number of stations and the number of jobs allowed at one station. In fact, the longer the ConWIP loop, the more cards are needed. There should be at least one job at each station to avoid starvation. This requires two cards when there are two stations, but 100 cards when there are 100 stations; the calculation is very simple: each job has one card and each station has one job. The two or 100 jobs could, however, also be queuing at just one station without the ConWIP system reacting since the limit is on the jobs in the system, not on the jobs at a particular station. To keep the limit per station at a reasonable level and achieve control, the number of stations in the loop should consequently be small.

This may mean that the line has to be broken down into segments that comply with the above three criteria, and this results in multiple ConWIP loops—as illustrated in Figure 6.4. But it is apparent that if the shop floor is segmented, then we gradually approach a *kanban* system, and we will consequently experience the same difficulties as for *kanban* systems with the propagation of information from the last segment to the first segment.

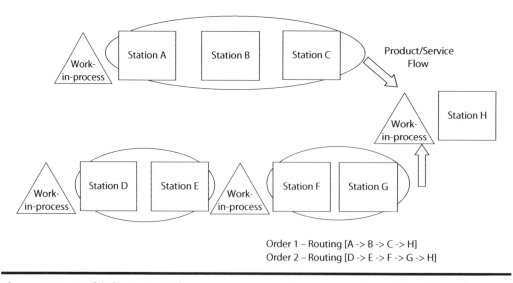

Order 1 – Routing [A -> B -> C -> H]
Order 2 – Routing [D -> E -> F -> G -> H]

Figure 6.4   Multiple ConWIP loops to accommodate two orders with different routings.

Finally, the fact that ConWIP only controls the number of jobs in the system also implies that ConWIP is highly sensitive to variability in processing times. The mix of jobs on the shop floor must balance the work across stations. Like a *kanban* system, ConWIP does not integrate workload balancing capabilities, and thus it should only be applied to shops with low processing time variability.

Summary: ConWIP

ConWIP overcomes the problems related to the propagation of information concerning what job should be processed next by the line that had been previously observed for *kanban* systems. This is achieved by sending a card from the end of the line directly to the start of the line (rather than propagating it backward from station to station). This is similar to the use of work-in-process and production *kanbans* in the internal supply chain.

We saw that the major difference between a ConWIP and a *kanban* system is that ConWIP cards are (job) anonymous—they relate to "a job" and not "this particular job or job type." As a consequence, cards signal that "a job has been finished" (and another job can start) rather than indicating that it is now time to "produce this particular job (again)." This shifts the decision concerning which job to produce from the end to the beginning of the line. While ConWIP is a powerful solution for the order control problem, it can only really be applied in the pure flow shop (i.e. where all orders visits all stations in the same sequence), since

1. A point where all jobs enter the shop floor and leave the shop floor is needed to allow for one loop.
2. The flow of work should not be split to keep the work-in-process limited.

Highlights Revisited

■ *We outline ConWIP and compare it to* kanban *systems.* ConWIP uses a single loop from the end of the line to the start of the line to feed back information. This is similar to the use of work-in-process and production *kanbans* in the internal supply chain. The difference is that ConWIP cards are anonymous, signaling that a job has been finished.

The decision concerning which job to start next is then taken by the start of the line. The single ConWIP loop for the whole line is often segmented into independent ConWIP loops. This segmentation leads to ConWIP approaching the *kanban* system.

■ *We discuss the applicability of ConWIP.* ConWIP is a simple, straightforward solution for the order control problem. However, it does not control individual stations; it only limits the number of jobs in the whole system. Therefore, it should only be applied in the pure flow shop with low processing time variability.

Chapter 7

Inventory Control Plus Material Requirements Planning for the Order Control Problem: POLCA

Highlights

- *We outline paired-cell overlapping loops of cards with authorization (POLCA) and compare it to the* kanban *and constant work-in-process (ConWIP) systems.*
- *We discuss the applicability of POLCA.*

A first solution to the order control problem has been presented in the previous chapter in the form of ConWIP. But we saw that it is restricted to the pure flow shop. ConWIP can be used to create multiple loops, but this transforms ConWIP back into a *kanban* system and, consequently, leads to the same problems of card propagation as with *kanban* systems. A different approach to solving the order control problem was presented in the form of paired-cell overlapping loops of cards with authorization (POLCA).

Paired-Cell Overlapping Loops of Cards with Authorization (POLCA)

This is a card-based control system that was first presented by Suri (1998) as part of Quick Response Manufacturing, a management philosophy that emphasizes short lead times and quick response to customer demand. POLCA essentially combines a material requirements planning (MRP) system (to provide a signal to all stations) with the card-based loop structure of a *kanban* system.

This chapter will explore how POLCA works, particularly its card-based component. But let's first clarify that we talk about stations instead of cells (as is more typical in the POLCA literature) to keep it consistent with the rest of this book. In fact, when we defined stations in a process at the beginning of the book, we saw that the boundary is not fixed. The difference between a machine, station, work center, cell, etc. is one of perspective or level of analysis—it does not affect the functioning of the card-based control system. In fact, *kanban* systems were already being used to link cells together in the early 1980s (Monden 1983). So we will continue to use the term "station"—but this could equally be replaced by "cell," or something else.

POLCA: How Does It Work?

POLCA is not a pure card-based system like, for example, *kanban*. Rather it requires an MRP system to calculate earliest release dates for each operation. These earliest release dates are used to prioritize when to start producing on the shop floor.

Earliest Release Date (POLCA)

Determines when an operation can be started at the station at which the operation is executed. It is called a release date since transformed resources are waiting in the queue in front of each station and are released from this queue. The earliest release date is determined by a material requirements planning (MRP) system.

Material Requirements Planning

Developed by Joseph Orlicky (e.g. Orlicky 1975) in response to the Toyota Production System. It uses coordination by plan.

Thus, with POLCA each transformed resource (part, product, etc.) has an earliest release date for each operation in its process, which determines when a station in its routing can start executing the operation. This release date is calculated by an MRP system. This raises a question—what is the difference between MRP and POLCA? After all, doesn't POLCA use the same scheduled dates for each operation as MRP? The main difference is that, in POLCA, cards are used to signal current capacity availability—a station is not authorized to work on an order if capacity is not available. So POLCA extends MRP by a capacity control element based on mutual adjustment.

Timeout: The need to be supported by MRP is a major drawback of the POLCA system. It requires an MRP system for calculating the earliest release date—and the system itself is extremely sensitive to this calculated date. We will see that, if the earliest release dates calculated by the MRP system are too late, the system may in fact end up starving since a station is not authorized to start working on a transformed resource if its release date has not been reached.

In a POLCA system, card loops are established between stations/cells/work centers/machines. POLCA cards operating within a loop are specific to a loop. For example, an A-B card will circulate between Station A and Station B. We will now describe how this loop is established.

When Station A is scheduled to start to work on a transformed resource *destined* for Station B (based on the earliest release date calculated by the MRP system), it requires a POLCA card from the loop A-B. If the POLCA card A-B is available, it is attached to the transformed resource and the order is processed at Station A. Overall, four things are needed to start an operation in POLCA:

1. The transformed resource must have arrived at Station A.
2. Station A must be available.
3. The earliest release date for this transformed resource at Station A must have been reached.
4. The POLCA A-B card must be available, indicating the future availability (of capacity) at Station B.

Once the operation at Station A is completed, the order moves to Station B (always with the A-B POLCA card attached). This is illustrated in Figure 7.1.

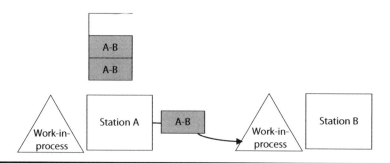

Figure 7.1   A POLCA card A-B is attached to the order, the order is processed and moves to Station B.

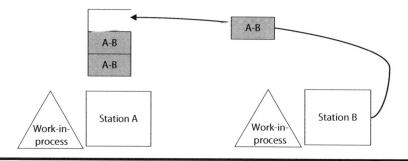

Figure 7.2   Once the operation at Station B is completed, the POLCA A-B card is sent back to Station A.

The order enters the queue at Station B and awaits the execution of its operation at Station B. Once the operation at Station B is completed, then and *only then* is the A-B card sent back. In other words, the card is attached to the transformed resource from the beginning of its operation at Station A until the end of its operation at Station B. Sending back the card to Station A closes the loop, as illustrated in Figure 7.2.

Timeout: This description follows the one typically encountered in the POLCA literature. Let's look at the same process from the perspective of a kanban *system. Kanban systems would typically be described from the perspective of the later station, i.e. Station B in our example. But let's describe it from the earlier station perspective. Imagine the same transformed resource but now we have no MRP system to calculate an earliest release date. So it has the highest priority. To start working on this transformed resource destined for Station B, it requires a* kanban *card from Station B. If this* kanban *card A-B (since it belongs to the loop A-B) is available, it is attached to the transformed resource and the order is processed at Station A. Overall, four things are needed to start an operation in a* kanban *system:*

- The transformed resource must have arrived at Station A;
- Station A must be available;
- It must be the order with the highest priority (e.g. determined by the dispatching rule); and
- The *kanban* A-B card from Station B must be available, indicating the future use (of capacity) at Station B.

Once the operation at Station A is completed, the order moves to Station B (always with the A-B *kanban* card attached). The order enters the queue at Station B and awaits the execution of its operation at Station B. Once the operation at Station B has started, then and only then is the A-B card sent back.

The main difference between a POLCA loop and a *kanban* loop is that a POLCA card is freed as soon as the operation is *completed* at the second station; meanwhile, in a *kanban* loop, it is freed as soon as the operation is *started* at the second station (since it signals its use).

There are some extremely important points being touched upon here:

- There should be at least two POLCA cards per loop to avoid starvation—i.e. to allow for one card at Station A and one at Station B—since each loop contains two operations that must be executed at these stations.
- A POLCA card signals that there is capacity at the next station in the routing of the order. It is argued, e.g. by Suri (2010), that this is different from a *kanban* card, which signals backward that a transformed resource was used and should be replenished. In fact, what the POLCA card does is tell Station A: "We finished one of the jobs you sent us; you can send us another" (Suri 2010, pp. 133–134). This is exactly what a *kanban* card does when going to the preceding process to withdraw a transformed resource—but the *kanban* says "we used that last job you sent us" not "we finished one of the jobs."
- Like ConWIP, POLCA cards are (job) anonymous—referring to "one of the jobs." Anonymous means that the card itself does not reveal which job it refers to. In fact, it is argued that they represent capacity and are not linked to any specific transformed resource (part, order, etc.) or any specific operation. This means they avoid the problem of direct and indirect work. A major function of *kanban* cards is identification to ensure the right transformed resources are used. POLCA loses this capability of identification. This is why POLCA needs an MRP system.

The main function of the MRP system is to ensure the right transformed resources (in terms of earliest release date) are worked on.

■ It is often argued that POLCA is different from *kanban* since an A-B card in POLCA tells us something about the availability of capacity at B while also making sure we make the best use of capacity at A. For example, if a job for A-B and a job (of similar urgency) for A-C are waiting and capacity is available at A, then processing the A-B job is a better use of capacity at A because the presence of the A-B cards means we know that the job will be needed at B soon; the A-C job may just add to the queue at C. If we look at it from a *kanban* perspective, then *kanban* simply does not signal from C to A but rather from B to A, since a part is not used if there is no capacity. So, POLCA and *kanban* share the same loop although they are described from a different perspective—POLCA as checking forward and *kanban* as signaling backward. In both cases, using either a *kanban* card from B or a POLCA A-B card, it is signaled that a job is needed at the next station.

Applicability of POLCA

We saw that there are three main differences between a *kanban* and a POLCA system:

■ In POLCA, cards are (job) anonymous—they are not bound to a specific transformed resource and its resource requirements, as is the case for *kanbans*.
■ POLCA requires an MRP system for calculating earliest release dates, i.e. the earliest date when an operation can be started at a station, which is required since cards are anonymous.
■ In POLCA, an operation cannot start if its earliest release date has not been reached, while no such restriction exists in *kanban* systems.

The fact that cards are anonymous creates the need for the MRP system. It is now signaled that a station has capacity but not what it shall work on (i.e. how it will use that capacity)! A POLCA system without earliest release dates for the prioritization of transformed resources waiting in the queue of a station may easily result in a system that produces only unneeded products/services, since there is no information concerning what is needed.

Timeout: The cards in POLCA just say that there is capacity at a station. They don't say what it should be used for. This is similar to ConWIP cards. It is the main difference with the kanban *system. In fact, the card-based element of POLCA can arguably be interpreted as a* kanban *system with ConWIP cards (in the sense that cards are (job) anonymous).*

The information that is needed is provided by the earliest release date—from the higher-level MRP system. But this introduces the weakness of a push system, and POLCA is highly sensitive to any inaccuracies in the calculated earliest release dates. For example,

1. *The calculated earliest release date is too late*: although transformed resources are available, stations may remain idle because the operation cannot take place since the earliest release date has not yet been reached, leading to unnecessary starvation.
2. *The calculated earliest release date is too early*: the prioritization of work is severely affected since it is less clear which order is the most urgent (all orders are urgent).

You might now be wondering: Why make cards anonymous? In fact, what POLCA actually does is to use an inventory control system for order control. If we only look at the card-based part of POLCA—ignoring MRP—we see a chain of decoupled POLCA card loops. Since cards are anonymous, each loop is decoupled from the previous and succeeding loop. Meanwhile, these loops are coupled by a centralized MRP system using earliest release dates, as illustrated in Figure 7.3.

When, in a *kanban* system, Station C needs to communicate to Station A that it should work on a specific order, it needs to signal to Station B, which in turn needs to signal to Station A. We discussed above why this propagation of information from station to station is a major headache of a *kanban* system in the context of an order control problem. In a POLCA system (where no information on job characteristics is propagated since cards are [job] anonymous), this signal is provided by a centralized MRP system. This makes the POLCA system well suited to the order control problem.

Timeout: POLCA card loops share no information on which order to start. This means that they are decoupled from each other. The only indication of prioritization is provided by the earliest release dates calculated by the MRP

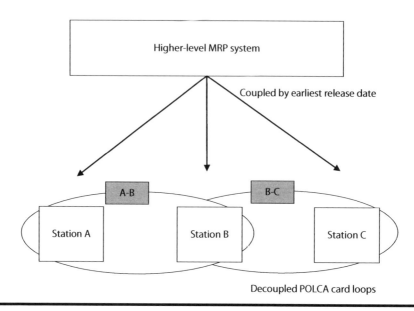

Figure 7.3   Decoupled POLCA card loops coupled by MRP.

system. So, rather than selecting a specific job (as in a kanban *system), POLCA only considers the urgency of jobs. The coupling of the decoupled POLCA loops by MRP only occurs in the time dimension. This is justified by the fact that POLCA was originally developed as a technique for achieving some of the principles of Quick Response Manufacturing, a management philosophy that emphasizes short lead times and quick response to customer demand. Information about what kind of operation is needed, i.e. should be executed by the station, still needs to be conveyed in another form. In contrast to a pro-duction* kanban, *which can function as a work order that details each pro-cess step, POLCA cards do not provide any such information. Hence, POLCA loops are just coupled in time not in work content.*

Since POLCA and *kanban* share the same physical loop structure, the same restrictions on the routing apply. All possible routing steps for orders flowing through the shop floor require a POLCA loop to be set up in advance, which means high routing variability leads to a large number of loops that are cumbersome to handle. Therefore, one should only apply POLCA when routings are simple. Another important shortcoming is that POLCA leads to blocking if there is undirected routing. An example routing characteristic that is prone to blocking is given in Figure 7.4, while Figure 7.5 illustrates the blocked system. As a result, POLCA should only be applied to shops with a directed routing.

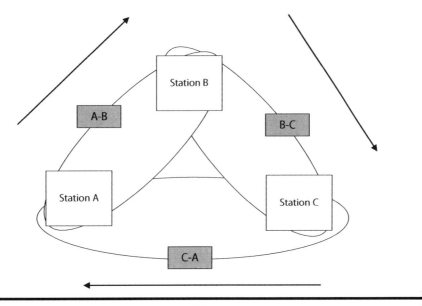

Figure 7.4   A POLCA system prone to blocking.

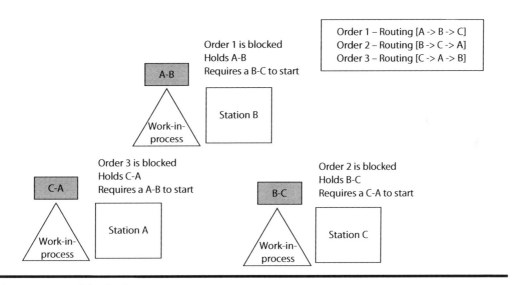

Figure 7.5   A blocked POLCA system.

Blocking (in the Context of POLCA)

This means that one station (say Station A) cannot start working on an order because another station (Station B) holds the POLCA card it needs, yet Station B cannot start working to free the POLCA card required at Station A because it requires a POLCA card from Station A—stalemate!

Timeout: You may ask, if kanban *loops and POLCA loops are so similar (or even equal)—why would* kanban *not block? What we have here is an order control problem. If* kanban *is used in an order control problem, then we saw earlier that the signal from the last to the first station has to be propagated from station to station. So a card associated with the indirect load of the order at each station should be waiting at each station. The problem with POLCA is that it transforms an order control problem into an inventory control problem. You will have noticed that POLCA cards never represent indirect load.*

Meanwhile, in an inventory control problem, jobs are interchangeable, so a situation such as the one depicted in Figure 7.5 cannot arise. Since all three orders have a specific routing, they are apparently not interchangeable.

If we want to transform the problem in Figure 7.5 into an inventory control problem for a kanban *system, we need at least three different* kanbans *(one for each job). This was a major criticism put forward against* kanban—*each specific order/part requires at least one* kanban. *However, it may in fact be easier to transform the problem into an inventory control problem. This may increase the inventory (since inventory for each order needs to be held), but it significantly simplifies the control problem. Remember that the inventory/ order separation point is your decision. Like always—a balanced decision has to be made taking all possibilities into account.*

Finally, as for *kanban* and ConWIP systems, POLCA does not incorporate any workload balancing capabilities. This hinders its application when processing time variability is high. In other words, POLCA does not create a mix of jobs on the shop floor that levels the workload across stations. As with a *kanban* system, POLCA keeps load information local. Moreover, processing time information is not provided, since POLCA cards are anonymous.

Summary: POLCA

Like *kanban*, POLCA uses card loops between stations. However, different from the various *kanban* systems, POLCA cards are (job) anonymous. As with ConWIP cards, POLCA cards signal that work has been completed and that new work destined for this station can be started—but they do not specify what work. This decouples each POLCA loop. However, it remains unknown which job should be worked on next. In fact, if POLCA card loops were used in isolation, each station could theoretically work on an order that is not needed. To ensure only needed work is completed, POLCA is supported by an MRP system. The MRP system calculates an earliest release date for each operation. This ensures that only urgent orders are worked on. However, the introduction of an MRP system introduces the flaws connected with push systems—a high sensitivity to inaccuracy in the calculated release date. In fact, if the earliest release date is too late, additional starvation is introduced since an operation cannot start at a station if the earliest release date has not been reached (even if the station is starving). Meanwhile, if earliest release dates are too early, all orders become urgent, which hinders accurate prioritization. POLCA allows for higher routing variety than ConWIP, but we saw that feedback loops in the loop structure may result in blocking.

Highlights Revisited

- *We outline POLCA and compare it to the* kanban *and ConWIP systems.* POLCA integrates two elements: (i) a card-based element for capacity control; and (ii) an MRP (or scheduling) based element for the prioritization of work. The card-based element shares the same loop structure as a *kanban* system, but POLCA cards are (job) anonymous. In this sense, they are similar to ConWIP cards.
- *We discuss the applicability of POLCA.* Since POLCA cards are anonymous, stations are decoupled. This avoids the issues with card propagation that jeopardize the application of *kanbans* to the order control problem. However, it requires an MRP system to prioritize orders since cards provide no information on which order to process next and the POLCA system is highly sensitive to the accuracy of these earliest release dates. POLCA is a solution to the order control problem, which allows for higher routing variability than ConWIP. However, it may lead to blocking if the routing is not directed. As for *kanban* systems, card loops have to be established for every possible routing step. Therefore, it should only be applied in shops with low routing variability. Finally, POLCA does not integrate load balancing and should consequently only be applied in shops with low processing time variability.

Chapter 8

How to Solve the High Variety Order Control Problem: COBACABANA

Highlights

- *We outline control of balance by card-based navigation (COBACABANA) and compare it to other card-based systems.*
- *We discuss how COBACABANA supports load balancing.*
- *We discuss how the need for processing time estimations can be simplified.*
- *We discuss the importance of avoiding unnecessary or premature idleness.*

Let's summarize what we have learned so far about card-based systems (Chapters 5 through 7). First, *kanban* systems are a powerful tool in internal supply chains, where different convergent flows of products/services need to be coordinated. But a *kanban* system will only control the flow of independent product/service flows through the shop floor—i.e. shop floor control—if *kanban* loops are decoupled from each other. We characterized this kind of control as an inventory control problem. If a *kanban* system is used to control the flow of a specific order, we run into a problem with the propagation of information from station to station. In fact, in an order control problem, a *kanban* may represent not the direct load at a station but the indirect work still upstream and yet to arrive at the station. This means the second station should allow for twice as many *kanban* cards as the first station, the third station should allow three times as many cards as the first station, and so on. The further downstream we go, the more indirect load there is, and the more *kanban* cards have to be allowed for. Since a *kanban* system is controlled by the last station in the line, control becomes complex in an order control problem.

A simple solution to the order control problem was presented in the form of the constant work-in-process (ConWIP) system, which avoids the propagation of information from station to station by using only one loop between the last and the first station. However, this loop must reflect all possible routings, which means all orders have to enter the shop floor at the same station and leave the shop floor at the same station. Moreover, ConWIP just controls the number of jobs (and thus work) in the system—individual stations are not controlled. To control the work-in-process at individual stations, ConWIP should only be applied to a pure flow shop (i.e. where the flow of work is not split), and processing time variability should be low.

A different solution to the order control problem was presented by paired-cell overlapping loops of cards with authorization (POLCA). We saw that POLCA avoids the aforementioned problem with *kanban* by using (job) anonymous cards to represent capacity availability at a station. The anonymous cards decouple the loops. This transforms the order control problem into an inventory control problem where cards just present the direct load. In fact, POLCA's card-based system alone does not prescribe which order to produce next, since orders are not indicated. To prioritize orders, a higher-level material requirements planning (MRP) system is used. This MRP system calculates an earliest release date for each operation in the routing of an order—this seeks to ensure that only orders needed are worked on. However, it also makes the POLCA system highly sensitive to any inaccuracies in the calculated earliest release dates, thereby reintroducing the flaws of a push system.

It appears that while there are solutions for the order control problem, these solutions only apply to contexts with low variability in routing and processing times. This excludes many shops from the benefits of simple card-based control. But let's consider what a card-based control system for the order control problem should look like to make it suitable for high-variety contexts.

1. *Use an explicit pool that precedes the shop floor*: We saw that ConWIP avoids the propagation from station to station by using only one loop between the last and the first station, but this requires a fixed first station in the routing of all jobs. In high-variety settings, an explicit pool that precedes the shop floor could be used. Orders can then enter the shop floor at any station.

2. *Control the release of orders from the pool to the shop floor*: Orders could be released from the pool by a release function to meet certain performance targets, such as to limit work-in-process levels or to adhere to delivery lead times. For example, a work-in-process cap (WIP-Cap) could be set for each station, and each order could be considered for release according to some measure of urgency.

3. *Use feedback information from the shop floor to control release*: The release decision can be supported by information on the load situation at each work center, which is provided by card loops between each station on the shop floor and the central pool.

4. *Use the centralized information to create a mix of jobs on the shop floor that balances the workload across resources*: Having all load information in one place would allow for taking load balancing considerations into account, which accommodates processing time variability.

   This is the basic idea of the final card-based control system that we will examine in this chapter—COBACABANA.

Control of Balance by Card-Based Navigation (COBACABANA)

This system was developed by Land (2009). It is the card-based equivalent to workload control, a production control solution developed specifically for job shop environments. Workload control does not release work directly to the shop floor, but arriving orders have to wait in a pre-shop pool that precedes the shop floor. Orders are released from the pool so as to create a mix of orders on the shop floor that stabilizes the work-in-process across stations while realizing other performance targets, such as adherence to due dates. This release decision is supported by feedback on the current workload situation on the shop floor. Before being translated into a card-based system by Land (2009), workload control was typically implemented using some form of software solution.

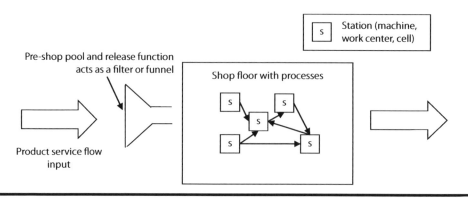

Figure 8.1 The pre-shop pool and release function act as a filter or funnel of work to the shop floor.

COBACABANA: How Does It Work?

COBACABANA establishes card loops between a central planner performing the release decision and each station on the shop floor. So it is different from other card-based systems that establish card loops between stations—it uses a central pool of work that precedes the shop floor. This allows for accommodating all possible routing characteristics. Orders are then released from this pool so workloads are balanced, and delivery dates are met. The pool and its release function act as a filter or funnel (as illustrated in Figure 8.1) that controls the work entering the shop floor.

Cards appear in *pairs* made up of (i) one release card per operation; and (ii) one operation card per operation. A card represents a certain workload amount according to its size. While the release card stays with the planner, each operation card travels with the order until the operation has been completed. The release cards are used for workload calculations at release while the operation cards are used to provide feedback on the current workload situation on the shop floor. The overall COBACABANA loop structure is illustrated in Figure 8.2.

Timeout: If an order has six operations then it has six operation cards at the first station in its routing. Once the first operation is finished, the corresponding card is sent back to the planner (signaling that the operation is complete), and the order moves on to the next station in its routing with five cards, and so on.

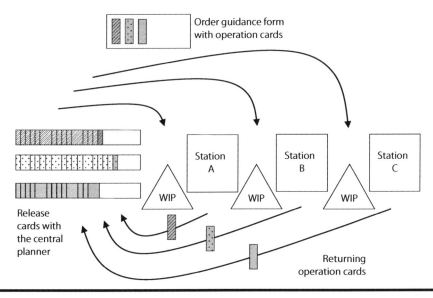

Figure 8.2   COBACABANA system—loops between the central planner and the stations on the shop floor.

The main differences between COBACABANA and a *kanban* system are:

1. COBACABANA loops are established between stations and a central release function, not between stations on the shop floor. This allows for accommodating all routing permutations.
2. Cards pertain to a station *and* an order (i.e. they represent a specific operation at a station).
3. Cards represent a workload amount (measured in processing time) based on the work required by the order's operation that is executed at that particular station.
4. The amount of workload is indicated by the size of the card.

The first difference (i) overcomes the problem of propagating information. The other three points (ii through iv) allow COBACABANA to balance the workload across stations as part of the release function.

Release decisions can either take place

- As soon as an operation is complete or new work arrives to the pool (i.e. continuously at any moment in time); or
- At set periodic time intervals.

Timeout: There is an example of a continuous release system that is often encountered at the airport during passport control. There are several counters, but people are not allowed to just line up at one of them. Rather, they have to wait in front of the space where the counters are (in a pool) and are released to the counters so the same amount of people is waiting in front of each counter. The officer typically releases people to the counter whenever the system state changes—continuously. An example of a periodic system is a typical traffic light system. At periodic time intervals, cars (orders) are released to the road (the shop floor). If traffic lights are used well, they help to stabilize the flow of cars through the system. While periodic traffic systems are common, there are some countries where you can turn right at an intersection at any time according to the current load situation (i.e. the presence of other cars crossing the intersection). This introduces a continuous release element; and, in these situations, periodic release and continuous release are combined to avoid "unnecessary" or premature idleness (i.e. a car turning right having to wait although the road ahead is empty).

Making release decisions on a continuous basis is generally recommended in a pure flow shop, while a more fixed, periodic approach is recommended in a job shop or general flow shop. Quite why this is the case will be explored later in the chapter when we discuss "unnecessary" idleness or starvation (and how it can be avoided). But let's introduce one means of avoiding starvation first—the main release function.

Timeout: We use the term "unnecessary" to highlight the fact that some idleness necessarily occurs if utilization is not 100% (and 100% utilization is only possible in a perfectly synchronized shop and thus an ideal type). What is important is to avoid starvation if there is work waiting that needs to be done—this is also called premature idleness in the literature and will be discussed in more detail later in this chapter.

Balancing Workloads: The Main Order Release Function of COBACABANA

The objective of the main release function of COBACABANA is to create a mix of jobs on the shop floor that balances the workload across resources. This is achieved by selectively releasing orders from the pool so the workload across stations is kept within a limit or norm (a WIP-Cap).

To achieve this goal, the workload on the shop floor must somehow be measured—only then can it be controlled. Feedback loops of cards are used in COBACABANA to visualize the workload on the shop floor and to facilitate the release decision. But let's next see how the release decision works.

First, and to ensure the right orders are on the shop floor (e.g. the most urgent ones), orders in the pool are sorted according to a pool sequencing rule, as discussed in Chapter 3. Orders are then considered for release, beginning with the first order in the sequence.

The workload of the operation at each station in the routing of the order being considered for release is added to the load of the corresponding station(s). In other words, for each station in the routing of an order, a pair of release and operation cards is taken before the release card—of a size corresponding to the workload of the order at the particular station—is added to the workload of that station on the planner's planning board.

Planning Board

This simple board is used for the calculations required at order release. The workload released to each station that still needs to be processed is represented by the cards on the board.

This is illustrated in the example planning board depicted in Figure 8.3, which shows a new order with two operations being considered for release: one operation at Station B and one at Station C (in dark gray). Each order that is released to the shop floor and is yet to be fully processed at a

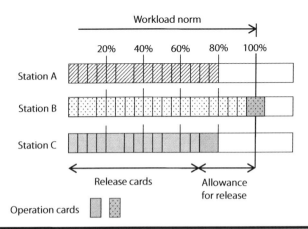

Figure 8.3   The planner's planning board for order release (with an example release decision).

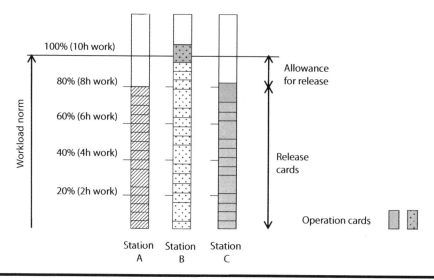

Figure 8.4   The planner's planning board with a workload norm of 10 hours turned 90° (a real-time Yamazumi board).

particular station has a release card corresponding to that station (of the appropriate size) held on the planning board. The bar, which is made up of all of the release cards of a station, therefore gives the direct load at a station (queuing and being processed) and the workload that is released to the shop floor and on its way to a station (the indirect load). This aggregate of the direct and indirect workload is what is controlled by COBACABANA. So, rather than controlling a number of cards, the workload represented by cards is controlled.

Timeout: Maybe the planning board is better understood by rotating it 90°, as illustrated in Figure 8.4. Now you can imagine each of the columns in front of the corresponding stations. Each of these columns represents the work (direct and indirect) currently released to a station. The workload is updated each time an operation is completed—as soon as an operation is completed, the operation card is sent back and the corresponding release card on the display is withdrawn. So COBACABANA's planning board works like a real-time Yamazumi board. You may ask why we don't represent the planning board in this way. Just try to take a card out from the middle!

Yamazumi Board

This is a stacked bar chart. The workload of individual operations at a station constitutes a bar. This bar represents the workload at or to a certain station.

When it is kept within a maximum workload limit (or the cycle time when used for line balancing), the workload across stations can be balanced.

The workload that can be released to a station (represented by the release cards) is limited by a WIP-Cap or workload norm.

Workload Norm (WIP-Cap)

This is a maximum limit on the workload released to a station (and thus on the shop floor). An important aspect of the workload norm is that it limits the workload (i.e. the amount of work to be processed at a station), not the number of jobs.

Keeping the workload within the workload norm controls it. If, for any station in the routing of an order, the workload represented by the release cards (the existing workload plus the workload of the new card) violates (i.e. exceeds) the 100% workload norm level, the order is retained in the pool, and the release cards of the order are removed. Otherwise, the release cards are assigned to all of the stations in the routing of the order, the corresponding operation cards are attached to the order guidance form of the order, and the order is released. In the example illustrated in figures 8.3 and 8.4, the order is not released because the workload norm is violated by the new workload contributions at Station B. This procedure is repeated until all orders in the pool have been considered once.

Order Guidance Form

This storage device accompanies each order through the whole production process. Its basic function is to store the COBACABANA cards. But it is also used to gather information on order progress or quality problems for later diagnosis.

Timeout: As it is defined in this chapter, the order guidance form is equal to the vinyl envelope used to store kanban *cards by Taiichi Ohno and others. However, its function can be easily extended. For example, one may summarize basic job information and use it as a data collector for later diagnosis. Workers can write the completion dates on it to allow for constructing throughput and order progress diagrams. Or workers can report on quality problems, thereby providing important data for total quality management.*

The planning board bears some similarity with a *heijunka* box. But a *heijunka* box is mainly a device to store *kanbans* for *future* production. COBACABANA's planning board actually supports load balancing decisions, since it provides a quick overview of the *current* situation on the shop floor.

Timeout: The heijunka *box represents the future workload of the shop floor (i.e. that currently in the pool)—not the current workload. The* kanbans *in the* heijunka *box relate to the jobs in the pool that are scheduled to be released in the future. An advantage of the* heijunka *box is that it highlights any delays in production; if there are delays, cards are not withdrawn. In contrast, the planning board in COBACABANA represents the current load situation on the shop floor. This allows for the creation of a mix of jobs on the shop floor that balances the workload across stations.*

In a COBACABANA system, the released workload is represented by available cards and the release possibilities by available space on the planning board. Hence, the board provides a useful, visual tool for understanding both the workload on the shop floor and the release possibilities from the pool. The set of release cards currently withdrawn for a specific order also provides information on the progress of that order on the shop floor.

So far we have looked at the release decision. The card loops only come into play after jobs are released. They are used to update the information on the planning board. If an order is released, it enters the shop floor together with its operation cards. This is illustrated in Figure 8.5.

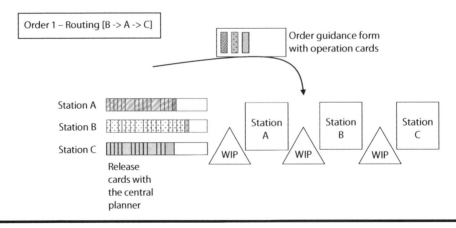

Figure 8.5   An order is released to the shop floor.

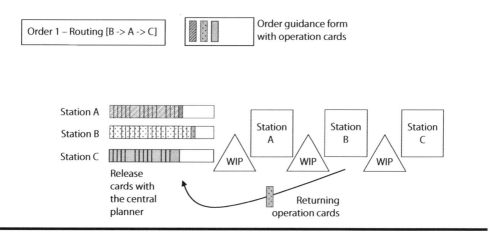

Figure 8.6 **The operation card signals to the central planner that the operation has been completed and that the release card should be withdrawn.**

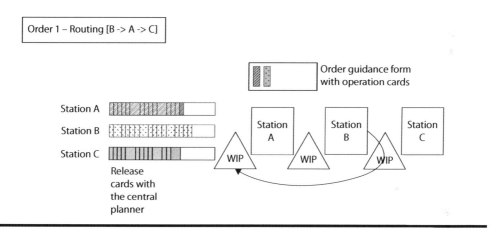

Figure 8.7 **The order moves on to the next operation until all operations are complete.**

As soon as an operation is completed, the operation card is sent back to the central release function, which formally signals its completion (see Figure 8.6). The release card corresponding to the operation card is then removed from the display. This closes the feedback loop.

If there are still operations to be completed, the order moves on to the next station, as illustrated in Figure 8.7, and so on.

COBACABANA Recognizes the Difference between Direct and Indirect Work

The load on the planning board represents the direct load currently queuing at a station and the indirect load that is still upstream, i.e. the load released but still on its way to the station. Together, the direct and indirect load is called the "aggregate load."

Aggregate Load (Used in COBACABANA)

This is the load released and still to be processed at a station. It is the aggregate of the direct load currently waiting in front of the station (the queue) or being processed and the indirect load, which is all of the workload that has been released to a station but has not yet arrived at the station (i.e. is still upstream).

Since this aggregate load represents all work on the shop floor yet to be transformed at a station (queuing/direct and upstream), a station positioned further downstream will need a higher workload norm than a station positioned further upstream. This is because it has to allow for the direct and (greater) indirect load.

To understand this, let's look at a pure flow shop where each order visits each station in the same sequence. Imagine we release three orders. So we have three release cards at each station. Now, when an operation is completed, the corresponding operation card comes back from the shop floor and signals the completion of this operation. The corresponding release card is withdrawn from the planning board. If one order is at each station, we see that each station has direct load queuing at the station and indirect load still at upstream stations (released from the pool but still on its way), as illustrated in Figure 8.8. The more downstream a station is positioned (and

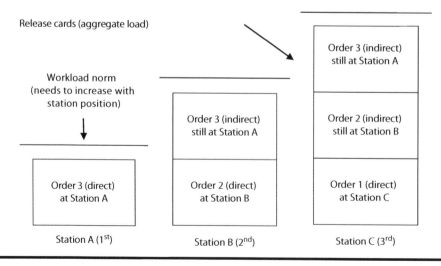

Figure 8.8   Release card distribution under the aggregate load measure.

the more upstream stations it has), the greater the indirect load. Therefore, if the workload norm is comprised of the aggregate of the direct and indirect load, it must be adjusted to compensate for this. In other words, it should be larger at downstream stations. Otherwise, a station will constantly go idle because it has reached its norm level but all of the work is upstream (indirect).

Timeout: The objective of COBACABANA is the creation of a mix of orders on the shop floor that stabilizes the workload across stations. This is achieved by selectively releasing orders to the shop floor. The stabilized workload needs of course to be the direct load, i.e. the load currently queuing at a station. So you may ask why we would consider the indirect load in the first place? Here is a counter-question: how would you consider just the direct load? When an order is released it can only add to the direct load of the first station in its routing. So we would neglect all the work it incurs at other stations—this load is still indirect. There is no problem if orders are standardized, meaning there is a strong correlation between the load at the first station in the routing and the load incurred at all other stations. In this case, just controlling one station controls all other stations. But if there is routing or processing time variability, then the system will be uncontrolled.

As in a *kanban* system, the further downstream a station is located, the more cards should be allowed. Thus, in COBACABANA, the further down-stream a station is, the higher the workload norm should be. This sounds easy if there is a directed routing, and, consequently, typical upstream and downstream stations can be identified. But what about a job shop (pure or restricted), where stations can have any routing position? One minute Station A is upstream in the mix of jobs released to the shop floor compared to Station B, and the next it is downstream, in an almost random sequence. This would require workload norms to constantly change. An alternative solution for the job shop is to adjust the workload contribution of each operation to a station rather than to adjust the norm of each station. The reasoning is very simple: if the second station requires two times the work-load norm of the first, why not set all workload norms the same and simply divide the workload contribution of a job to the second station by two? In other words, use the routing position to determine the workload contribu-tion and card size required—halve the workload (and card size) for the sec-ond station, divide it by three for the third station in the routing, and so on. This is illustrated in Figure 8.9.

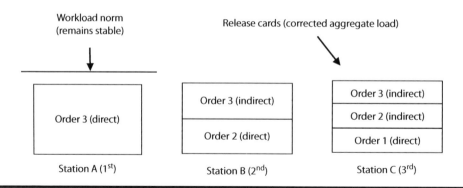

Figure 8.9 Release card distribution under the corrected load measure.

As each order contributes to all loads from the moment of release, correcting the workload in this way compensates for the fact that a job will only be part of the load queuing in front of the second station (i.e. direct load), for example, for around 50% of the time that it contributes. In other words, the cards related to the second station in the routing of an order go with the order at release and stay on the shop floor until the first two operations have been completed. Oosterman et al. (2000) showed how controlling this "corrected aggregate load" leads to stabilizing the direct load in front of a particular station.

Corrected Aggregate Load (Used in COBACABANA)

An order's workload contribution to each station in its routing is corrected by the position of this station in the routing of the order. This is a corrected measure of the aggregate load, which is specifically designed for use in job shops where routing characteristics constantly change.

Simplifying the Need for Processing Time Estimations

A COBACABANA card represents the workload of an order at a certain station. This workload may be measured either in aggregate load (i.e. full processing times) or in corrected aggregate load terms (i.e. the processing time corrected by the routing position of the station) according to the routing characteristics of the shop. At the time of order release, the cards can be cut to exactly the right size, representing the load contributions of the operations involved. However, we can also simplify the need for processing time estimations by limiting the number of card sizes. In this case, a card size represents a certain range of load contributions, rounded to the estimated average in that range. Thürer et al. (2014) recently showed that the use of only three card sizes—for small, medium, and large workload contributions—maintains most of the performance benefits of using a fully flexible card size. This means that processing times don't need to be estimated to the "millisecond" and cards don't have to be cut to the exact size each time.

What we mean is that rather than having to estimate that an operation takes 3 minutes and 11 seconds and to then have to cut the card to the corresponding size, we could just estimate that it takes around 3 minutes and that this is a typical medium-sized operation. Of course, this is context specific, and in another environment, 3 minutes could be a very small operation. Hence, what is small, medium, or large depends on what processing times look like in your shop.

Timeout: Many companies spend a lot of money and effort on estimating processing times (especially if they use software systems). But these estimates always have an error—especially in high-variety companies where an order may be being made for the first time. Sometimes operations will take longer than expected, and sometimes they will be quicker than expected. A big advantage of card-based systems compared to systems that use coordination by plan (e.g. MRP) is that they can cope with uncertainties and resulting estimation errors since they use feedback from the shop floor. But why, for example, try to estimate it to the millisecond if you know you have several seconds or more of error anyway? The results will be about equivalent if you just estimate all operation processing times that fall into some interval as being equal to the average of the interval, e.g. grouping all operations between 30 and 40 seconds as 35 seconds. In other words, processing time estimations should be simplified, recognizing that estimates have an error anyway.

COBACABANA and High Processing Time Variability: Starvation Avoidance

High variability in processing times will lead to an increased risk of unnecessary (or premature) idleness. This increased risk is independent of the control solution applied and will even occur in a shop with no control at all. Our focus here is on the means of mitigating the detrimental effect, i.e. on which counter-measures should be taken.

Starvation (or Idleness)

A transforming resource starves if it does not accomplish any transforming actions. This is a normal occurrence in most shops, since the only way to avoid starvation or idleness altogether is by maintaining a utilization level of 100%. A starving transforming resource is equivalent to waiting waste. But, as we have previously discussed, there may be times when it is better not to process than to process something that nobody wants.

Unnecessary (or Premature) Idleness

This is starvation, idleness, or inactivity that occurs when there is work that actually needs to be done.

Let's start by looking again at the pure flow shop. In a pure flow shop, all work arriving at a given station comes from one particular station. Hence, the work arriving is dependent on the processing times of orders at the preceding upstream station. Imagine an order waiting at Station A that has a processing time of 4 hours. If this order is now processed, no work will arrive at Station B for a further 4 hours. An inventory buffer of 4 hours of work will therefore be required to avoid Station B from running out of work. This is no problem if processing times are equal across orders. But imagine if the operation of the order at Station B takes just 30 minutes and not 4 hours. If there is one order at Station A and one order at Station B, the second station (Station B) will starve for 3 hours and 30 minutes. The problem is less severe in high-variety routings since work can also arrive from other stations. Still, it is an important source of bad performance.

Timeout: Remember that ConWIP and POLCA cards just represent a job, any job for that matter—without any further specification. So, in fact, a ConWIP card may on one occasion mean 4 hours of work for a station and on another occasion mean only 30 minutes of work—depending on the processing time variability of jobs. This is one reason why ConWIP and POLCA struggle in environments with high processing time variability. Another reason for bad performance in contexts with high processing time variability is that none of the "traditional" card-based systems create a mix of jobs on the shop floor that balances the workload across stations (i.e. that actually realizes heijunka). A major hindrance to the performance of kanban, ConWIP and POLCA is that no global view exists of the load situation on the shop floor, as is provided by COBACABANA's planning board.

Within COBACABANA, there are three main ways of avoiding unnecessary starvation:

1. Workload Balancing: The mix of jobs on the shop floor should be such that the load across stations is balanced.
2. Shortest Processing Time (SPT) Effects: Jobs with the shortest processing times at upstream stations can be prioritized to create the quickest replenishment of successive queues.
3. Work Injection: If a station is starving, an order with that particular station as the first in its routing is released from the pool regardless of the current workload situation. In other words, the corresponding release cards are assigned to the station in the routing of the order, the operation cards are attached to the order guidance form, and the order is released irrespective of whether a workload norm would be exceeded or not.

It is clear that the work injection solution becomes dysfunctional if there is only one station (the so-called gateway station) through which orders enter the process, as in the pure flow shop.

Gateway Station

If all orders enter the shop floor at one station, then this station is the gateway station.

Meanwhile, creating SPT effects has to be undertaken with care since giving priority to small orders means that large orders are postponed.

The above has important implications for the timing of the release decision, i.e. when the release decision should take place. In general, there are two rules to consider:

1. The release decision should be taken *periodically* if jobs may enter at any station (i.e. in job shops or the general flow shop). Using a periodic release interval allows large jobs to contribute to a balanced load since more capacity is available for each release decision than under a

continuous release approach. If jobs are released continuously up to a WIP-Cap, large jobs may be difficult to release (see the second point below). Starvation can be further avoided by injecting work (see, e.g. Thürer et al. 2012).

2. The release decision should be taken *continuously* whenever a new job arrives in the system, or an operation is completed in a pure flow shop. Here, the release function tends to fill up the workload norms on a continuous basis. This creates SPT effects if many jobs are waiting to be released because, for a job to fit the norm, its workload contribution has to be equal to or smaller than the workload contribution freed up by the job completed. While this may jeopardize the performance of large jobs, it is the main solution for avoiding starvation in this environment since the injection mechanism, which is restricted to the gateway station, becomes dysfunctional (see, e.g. Thürer et al. 2015).

Timeout: We talked about large jobs in this section. This refers to single orders with large processing times or lots/batches that cannot be split. Otherwise, reducing lot sizes will always be beneficial to improving load balancing, since it increases the granularity of the contributed load. It is therefore a key priority where possible—like reducing set-up times. But it is not always possible.

For example, POLCA seeks to avoid starvation through the introduction of a so-called quantum—i.e. a maximum amount of material that should accompany a single card. An uncommon or larger-than-typical order may consequently require more than one POLCA card (for a discussion, see Riezebos 2010). This presupposes that the large order can be broken down—only in this case will there be any effect. It is similar to the subdivision of large production batches into small transfer batches in Goldratt and Cox (2004).

Premature Station Idleness and Order Release

In this chapter, we discussed unnecessary idleness caused by processing time and/or routing variability. This idleness will always occur, even if no control is exercised. In fact, a major task for any production planning and control solution is the avoidance of unnecessary idleness. However, the WIP-Cap may introduce additional premature idleness.

The importance of avoiding premature idleness in the context of release methods that use a WIP-Cap was first recognized by authors such as Kanet (1988) and Land and Gaalman (1998). In this context, premature station idleness refers to a station (transforming resource) that is running idle even though resource requirements exist in the pool that could be released and processed directly at the station, i.e. without going to another station first. There are two sources of premature idleness or starvation:

1. When an order with the starving station in its routing has not been released due to a high workload at another station in its routing. In other words, the order cannot be released because it would lead to the workload norm of another station being exceeded.
2. When an order with the starving station in its routing has not been released because the starving station has a high indirect load, which makes the order violate the workload norm.

Timeout: If we look back at our pizza place, the cheese station may be starving (pardon the pun) even though there are pizzas waiting in the pool, because the dough station has a high workload and causes the workload limit to be violated. Now imagine we also produce lasagna, which (obviously) also requires the cheese station. Let's assume lasagna even starts at the cheese station—since our lasagnas only differ in terms of the type and amount of cheese put on them, the inventory/order interface is at the cheese station. Even lasagna may not be released to cheese although cheese is starving, simply because there are five pizzas upstream at dough causing a high indirect load at cheese. Now it would make sense to allow lasagnas to enter one by one until the first pizza dough is completed and arrives at cheese. This work (or lasagna) injection is an important means of overcoming premature station idleness.

The solution to both sources of premature idleness is work injection whenever a station is starving (see, e.g. Thürer et al. 2012). This means an order with the starving station as the first in its routing should be released regardless of its workload contribution. This recognizes the need to temporarily violate the 100% workload limit at a certain station to avoid premature idleness. As was the case for avoiding starvation due to processing time variability, this approach can only be applied if orders enter the process at different stations and can thus be injected. If there is a gateway station, injection should not be applied—the problem is however less severe if norms are set appropriately since the gateway station, as the most tightly controlled station, only has a direct load (any indirect load for this station would be in the pool, not on the shop floor).

Summary: COBACABANA

Control of balance by card-based navigation (COBACABANA) is the card-based equivalent to workload control, a production control solution developed specifically for high-variety job shop environments. The main difference between COBACABANA and other card-based systems is that (i) COBACABANA uses an explicit pre-shop pool, which precedes the shop floor (while the pool is realized at the first station in the process by other card-based systems); and (ii) COBACABANA considers the need to balance the workload. Since orders are released from a pre-shop pool, which precedes the shop floor, they can enter the shop floor at any station. Meanwhile, the release of jobs is controlled to create a mix of jobs on the shop floor that balances the workload across stations while meeting performance targets such as meeting delivery dates. The release function is supported by card loops that provide feedback from the stations on the shop floor. All loops contain the central release function. This gives a global rather than a local view of the workload situation on the shop floor, which supports workload balancing across stations. Workload balancing calculations are facilitated by COBACABANA's planning board and the fact that the size of a card represents the workload contribution of an order to a station. In uncertain environments, there will be an error in processing time estimations. Therefore, rather than seeking to estimate what cannot be estimated, the procedure for processing time estimation should be simplified. In most shops, COBACABANA can be implemented with just three card sizes, e.g. to represent typical small, medium, and large processing times. So COBACABANA allows for handling all possible routing permutations as well as high processing time variability.

Highlights Revisited

- *We outline COBACABANA and compare it to other card-based systems.* The main differences between COBACABANA and other card-based systems can be summarized as follows. First, COBACABANA uses an explicit pre-shop pool that precedes the shop floor. This allows for orders entering the shop floor at any station. Second, card loops are established between stations and the pool. This decouples the routing and loop structure and allows all possible routing permutations to be accommodated. Third, orders are released from the pool to the shop floor so as to balance the workload across resources; and this accommodates processing time variability. Overall, COBACABANA represents a simple yet effective solution for the high variety order control problem.

■ *We discuss how COBACABANA supports load balancing.* A planning board is used to visualize the workload on the shop floor. This workload is represented by release cards, where each release card represents the workload contribution of an order to a station according its size; each card represents one operation. Operation cards circulate between each station and the pool providing feedback on operation completion. An order is only released if its workload does not cause the workload at any station in its routing to violate its workload norm. Keeping the workload represented by the release cards within norms controls the workload on the shop floor. The workload measure that is controlled relates to the entire load released to the shop floor and yet to be processed at a station, i.e. both the direct and indirect loads, known as the aggregate load. But this requires a constantly changing workload norm if routings vary, i.e. in a job shop. An alternative is to control a corrected measure of the aggregate load—for this measure, the workload contribution accounts for the routing position of a station. It is given by dividing the processing time by the routing position of a station rather than by taking the full processing time.

■ *We discuss how the need for processing time estimations can be simplified.* While the workload contribution (i.e. the full or corrected processing time according to the workload measure applied) can be represented exactly by cutting a card so that its size is proportionate to its processing time, this is not typically required. Rather, the need for processing time estimations can be simplified by limiting the number of card sizes. In this case, a card size represents a certain range of load contributions, rounded to the estimated average in that range. The use of only three card sizes—for small, medium, and large workload contributions—maintains most of the performance benefits of using a fully flexible card size.

■ *We discuss the importance of avoiding unnecessary or premature idleness.* All transforming resources will be starving or idle for some of the time (except if they are 100% utilized, which seems unlikely or even unadvisable, as it makes resources and the system vulnerable to disruption). However, this starvation should not occur if there is work that actually needs to be done. One reason for unnecessary starvation is processing time variability. COBACABANA provides three means of avoiding this type of starvation: workload balancing, SPT effects, and work injection. Unnecessary (or premature) idleness may also be introduced by the release method. For example, a job that will contribute directly to the load of a starving station upon its release may be held back in the pool due to the load situation at another station. The main means of avoiding this kind of starvation is work injection. In other words, whenever a station is going to starve, an order with this station as the first in is routing can be released from the pool, regardless of its load contribution to other stations.

Chapter 9

COBACABANA's Card-Based System for Delivery Time Estimation

Highlights

- *We outline a simple yet effective approach to delivery time estimation.*
- *We discuss control of balance by card-based navigation (COBACABANA) as a comprehensive concept.*
- *We discuss the use of the salesperson's display for output control (i.e. guiding capacity adjustments).*

In Chapter 4, we saw that a process may be either to-stock or to-order. If it is to-stock then the operations (i.e. the transformation of transformed resources) occur before the resource requirements are known. The customer expects the product/service to be there when he/she arrives. If it is to-order then the operations (i.e. the transformation of transformed resources) occur after the resource requirements. The customer is always waiting! This means that an allowance for the waiting time, also known as a delivery time allowance, is required.

Delivery Time Allowance

The time that the customer is willing to wait for the delivery of the product/service. This relates to the time between a customer making his/her requirements known (placing the demand) and receiving the product/service.

This delivery time allowance should be:

■ Competitive, i.e. agreeable to the customer (and therefore at least comparable with the delivery time allowance of other shops).
■ Realizable or feasible, i.e. the company should be able to provide the product/service within the allowance given the available transformed/ transforming resources and other resources requirements potentially competing for the same resources.

The estimation of competitive yet feasible delivery time allowances is a major task if production/service processes are to-order. Yet, until recently, card-based systems have remained limited in scope. They have only been used for controlling work on the shop floor. They do not typically support higher-level planning tasks, such as estimating delivery dates during customer enquiry management. This limits the advantage of using a simple, card-based control system, as it means companies have to maintain some other sophisticated planning and control processes to support these tasks. A simple solution for determining competitive yet feasible delivery time allowances will be presented in this chapter. This is the first and, to the best of our knowledge, only card-based solution for delivery time estimation. It was originally presented by Land (2009) as part of COBACABANA. Yet, in theory, this procedure could also be combined with *kanban*, constant work-in-process (ConWIP), or paired-cell overlapping loops of cards with authorization (POLCA).

Timeout: Determining realistic delivery times is the first step towards bridging the commonly encountered production/sales divide caused by the conflicting objectives of these two functions. On the one side, there is Sales—who want to maximize revenue by quoting often unrealistically short delivery times and prices. On the other side, there is Production—who push for a high backlog of work and longer delivery lead times to create a continuous flow on the shop floor. We know where our loyalties lie, but bridging this gap is key to the overall enterprise and to ensuring promises are made to customers that win their business but that can also be kept. This may be key to forming long-term relationships with customers and repeat business.

Card-Based Delivery Time Estimation: How Does It Work?

The card-based control systems that we have now come to know through Chapters 5 through 8 stabilize the work on the shop floor and consequently (following Little's Law), the shop floor throughput time—providing they are applied to the right control problem. This is achieved by separating the work accepted by the company into two parts: the work-in-process on the shop floor; and the work that is waiting to be released to the shop floor. Together, the two parts form the planned workload (see Chapter 2).

But the customer typically experiences the time from order acceptance through to delivery—and this is not the same as from release to delivery. Customers must wait for their orders to be first released and then processed; and their orders are likely to be waiting behind other orders that the company has taken on for other customers. The delivery time or due date allowance negotiated with the customer must consequently consider the lead time from order acceptance rather than the shop floor throughput time from order release. The lead time is the time that a job has to wait until release plus its shop floor throughput time (see Figure 9.1).

If operation throughput times and/or shop floor throughput times are stabilized by the card-based control system, then the only variable component of the deliver lead time is the time that a job has to wait in the pool prior to its release. We also add to these two components (one for the pool waiting time and one for the shop floor throughput time) another component that acknowledges that things don't always go to plan and allows for uncertainty (i.e. the variance of lateness). Lateness is given by the actual realized delivery date minus the planned delivery date. This third component is called the external allowance. So, overall, the delivery time allowance consists of three components (see Figure 9.2):

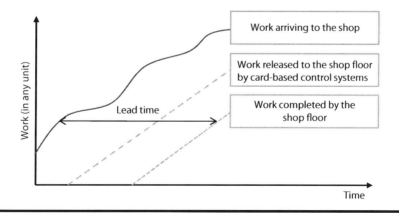

Figure 9.1   Illustrating why delivery time allowances should consider the lead time.

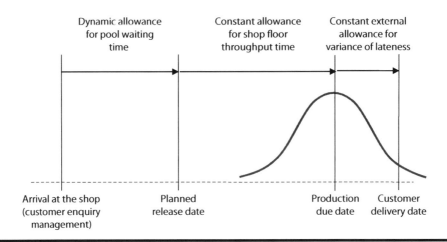

Figure 9.2   The three components of the delivery time allowance.

1. A dynamic allowance for the pool waiting time prior to release
2. A constant allowance for the shop floor throughput time, i.e. for the operation throughput time at each station in the routing of a job
3. A constant allowance for uncertainty, i.e. the variance of lateness or difference between the internally planned and actual delivery date

Timeout: It is important to recognize that card-based systems shift variability from the shop floor to the pool. Thus it will no longer be visible on the shop floor. The planner's display that is used in COBACABANA, which we discussed in the previous chapter, is a great means of visualizing workload fluctuations across stations if no norm or work-in-process cap is applied (and orders are released immediately without a pool delay). But as soon as a norm is applied, variability disappears from this display (since the represented workload is kept within norms) and moves into the pool. So we need a second device (the salesperson's display) to make the variability in the pool visible. This will be introduced next.

We assume that all of the variability in realized delivery times is explained by the time that jobs wait in the pool. This (reasonable) assumption significantly simplifies the task of estimating delivery time allowances. It means the only component that needs to be estimated to determine a competitive and feasible delivery time allowance is the pool waiting time.

To determine an allowance for the pool waiting time, card loops between customer enquiry management (where due dates are set by the salesperson) and the pre-shop pool are established.

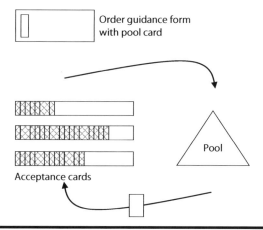

Figure 9.3   Card-based delivery date estimation—a card loop between customer enquiry management and order release.

Customer Enquiry Management

The function within a firm that negotiates with the customer, e.g. on price, delivery date, quantities, specifications, etc. It is here that the order acceptance decision is made. Customer enquiry management is typically part of Sales or sales and operations planning (S&OP).

Cards appear in pairs made up of one acceptance card per operation and one pool card per order, where acceptance cards represent different amounts of workload according to their size. While the acceptance card(s) stay with the salesperson, the pool card stays with the order until the order has been released. This basic loop structure is illustrated in Figure 9.3.

The main tool for determining the pool waiting time is the salesperson's display, as illustrated in Figure 9.4. This display shows the load waiting in the pool to be released to each station.

Salesperson's Display

This simple display is used for the calculations required at customer enquiry management (where delivery dates are set). The workload in the pool waiting to be released to each station is presented by the cards on the display. The rate at which work is released is given by the scale.

A minimum pool waiting time can be estimated based on Little's Law and using the work waiting in the pool to be released to the most constrained

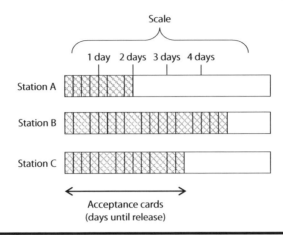

Figure 9.4 The salesperson's display for due date estimation at customer enquiry management.

station (i.e. the station in the job's routing with the largest load in the pool) and the average release rate of this station (i.e. the maximum output per time unit). In other words, the pool waiting time is given by the maximum pool load (given by the cards on the display) divided by the maximum output (or release) rate of the corresponding station (given by the scale).

Let's take a look at COBACABANA's whole customer enquiry management procedure, which can be put in place to complement the order release and shop floor dispatching procedure outlined in the previous chapter.

1. When an order arrives at the shop (i.e. customer enquiry management), a feasible delivery date is determined by adding the following three components to the current date: (i) the allowance for the pool waiting time derived from the salesperson's display; (ii) the allowance for the operation throughput times on the shop floor (which are stabilized by order release, i.e. each station has a specified throughput time that is regulated or maintain through controlled order release); and (iii) a so-called external allowance to account for variability—things don't always go to plan.
2. The order then contributes to the pool load of each station in its routing. In other words, for each station in the routing of an order, a card of a size corresponding to the workload of the order at a particular station is added to the workload of that station on the salesperson's display, the pool card is attached to the order guidance form, and the order moves into the pool to await release.

3. Once the order has been released, the pool card moves back to customer enquiry management, and the corresponding acceptance cards are withdrawn. This closes the feedback loop.

Finally, as for COBACABANA's order release procedure, only three different card sizes—to distinguish between small, medium, and large operations—are needed to obtain most of the performance benefits. This simplifies the need for processing time estimations at customer enquiry management (or sales).

Timeout: The delivery date estimation procedure described here can in fact sometimes be seen in pizza places. When a customer orders a pizza, a note is made on a sheet of paper, and the sheet of paper is put in a special place in the kitchen. This is the pool. The clerk at the counter uses the easily visible sheets of papers in the pool to estimate how long a pizza for a new customer will take.

COBACABANA as a Comprehensive System

A basic assumption for applying the simple card-based procedure for estimating competitive yet feasible delivery time allowance is that operation throughput times on the shop floor are stabilized and thus easily predictable. This transforms the task of delivery time estimation to only having to estimate the pool waiting time, which should be simpler. However, for it to work, the procedure needs to be combined with a card-based control system for stabilizing operation throughput times. In theory, this procedure could be combined with *kanban*, ConWIP, or POLCA, but there are two key reasons why COBACABANA's order release procedure is the preferred choice:

■ COBACABANA's order release solution is the most appropriate procedure for the high variety order control problem, which is typically prevalent in the kind of shop that needs support for estimating delivery time allowances (e.g. make-to-order shops producing customized products where standard lead times cannot be quoted).
■ The due date estimation procedure was presented as an extension to COBACABANA's release procedure by Land (2009), and so it is a natural fit.

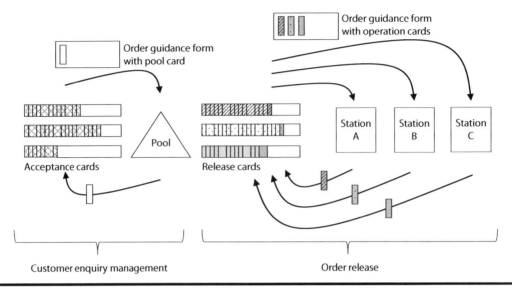

Figure 9.5 Integrated COBACABANA card-based solution—card loops between the salesperson at customer enquiry management and order release, and between the planner at order release and shop floor work centers.

The overall COBACABANA system—integrating due date estimations with order release control—is illustrated in Figure 9.5.

The first card loop is between customer enquiry management and the pre-shop pool. The acceptance cards for each operation represent the pool load, which is used to calculate due dates on the salesperson's display. The corresponding pool card moves with the order and allows the information flow to be established. When the order is released from the pool, the pool card returns to the salesperson's display, and the respective acceptance cards are removed.

The set of loops used for controlling the workload on the shop floor is from the pool to each station on the shop floor. Release cards are used to represent the shop floor workload on the planning board. The planning board is used by the planner for selecting jobs for release and facilitates load balancing calculations. Operation cards move with the order and allow the information flow to be established. When an operation is completed, the corresponding operation card is returned to the planning board and the corresponding release card is withdrawn. Finally, the different card types used in a comprehensive COBACABANA system are summarized in Table 9.1.

Table 9.1 Summary of the Different Card Types Used in COBACABANA

	Acceptance Card	*Pool Card*	*Release Card*	*Operation Card*
Where used?	Customer enquiry management		Order release control	
For what?	Represents the workload of a station in the pool on the salesperson's display	Creates the feedback loop between customer enquiry management and order release from the pool	Represents the shop floor workload of a station on the planner's display	Creates the feedback loop between order release from the pool and each station
How many?	One per operation; card size represents the workload contribution	One per job	One per operation; card size represents the workload contribution	One per operation

Using the Salesperson's Display for Output Control

We established at the start of this book that the basic idea underlying all card-based systems is input/output control, i.e. the input of work is aligned with the output. All card-based systems focus on input control. So, some tool for output control should also be applied to support them.

The main tool for output control is (increasing) the overall equipment effectiveness (OEE). Figure 9.6 provides a summary of how the OEE is defined.

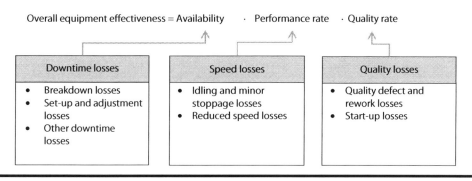

Figure 9.6   Overall equipment effectiveness.

This book is not the place to discuss how the OEE can be increased. But it is the place to highlight that this is an important tool. A second tool for output control is capacity adjustments. Indeed, there are several ways in which capacity can be adjusted, for example:

- If operators are assigned to more than one machine, the number of machines that an operator uses can then be adjusted to influence the output rate.
- Capacity can be redistributed or shifted, for example by reallocating capacity (i.e. operators) from an under-loaded to an overloaded station.
- Overtime can be used, although this can be costly, during high load periods.
- Work can be subcontracted/outsourced during overload periods.

Further information on all of these means of adjusting capacity can be found in the literature. For the purposes of this book, it is not so important as to *how* capacity is adjusted, but *when* and *where* (i.e. at which station) it is adjusted. In fact, only small adjustments are required if they are timely and at the right point—capacity adjustments should also be just-in-time (see, e.g. Land et al. 2015). This is why Taiichi Ohno stated that a major feature of the Toyota Production System is that decisions on overtime should be taken by workers at the lowest possible level (Ohno 1988, pp. 29, 45).

Capacity adjustments are most effective if there is a high load in the system. So the best means of deciding when and where capacity should be adjusted is the load situation at each station. This means if the *planned* workload for a certain station exceeds a certain threshold, capacity should be adjusted.

If the load at each station is stabilized, then the planned workload of each station is reflected in the salesperson's display. This display can therefore be used to guide decisions on capacity adjustments. The basic idea is illustrated in Figure 9.7.

Capacity adjustments can now also be effectively used to improve the competitiveness of delivery time negotiation. If the customer wants a shorter delivery time, required capacity adjustments can be derived from the salesperson's display. This then allows for calculating eventual costs incurred and how a shorter delivery time should be reflected in the price.

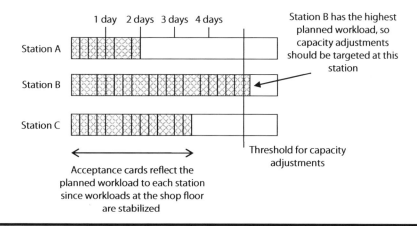

Figure 9.7   The salesperson's display for guiding capacity adjustments.

Summary: COBACABANA's Delivery Date Estimation Procedure

The estimation of competitive yet feasible delivery time allowances is a major task if production/service processes are to-order. Yet card-based systems have remained limited in scope. They have been used for controlling work on the shop floor, but they do not typically support other higher-level planning tasks, such as estimating delivery dates during customer enquiry management. This limits the advantage of using a simple, card-based control system, as it means companies have to maintain some other sophisticated planning and control processes to support these tasks. However, Land (2009) included a simple extension to COBACABANA that uses cards to estimate delivery times or due dates.

In Land's (2009) concept, the main tool for delivery time estimations is the salesperson's display. Similar to the planner's display at release, which makes the shop floor workload visible, the salesperson's display visualizes the workload in the pool that is waiting to be released to a certain station. Using Little's Law, this workload can be used to estimate pool waiting times. Since the workload on the shop floor is stabilized, the pool waiting time can be considered the only variable component of the lead time. Delivery time estimates can therefore be based on the sum of the estimate of the pool waiting time, a constant allowance for the shop floor throughput time, and an external allowance that accounts for variability between estimated and eventually realized delivery times.

Only focussing on the pool waiting time significantly simplifies the task of estimating delivery time allowances.

Highlights Revisited

- ■ *We outline a simple yet effective approach to delivery time estimation.* If a production/service process is to-order, a competitive yet feasible delivery time needs to be negotiated with the customer. This delivery time allowance can be broken down into three parts: an allowance for the pool waiting time, an allowance for the shop floor throughput time, and an external allowance for variability between the realized and estimated delivery time. COBACABANA's card-based delivery time estimation procedure assumes only the pool waiting is variable, since the shop floor throughput time is stabilized by the release method. To estimate the dynamic pool waiting time allowance for each order, the workload in the pool waiting to be released to a station is divided by the release rate (following Little's Law). To obtain a measure of the pool load of a station, card loops are established between the pool and customer enquiry management.

- ■ *We discuss COBACABANA as a comprehensive concept.* While the delivery time estimation procedure outlined here can be applied to any shop floor control system that stabilizes the shop floor throughput times, it is especially suitable for combining with COBACABANA's order release procedure, which is the most appropriate solution for high-variety to-order shops. It is these shops that are typically in most need of improved delivery time estimations. Moreover, the procedure is an extension of COBACABANA's release procedure—hence, it is the obvious, logical choice.

- ■ *We discuss the use of the salesperson's display for output control (i.e. guiding capacity adjustments).* Capacity adjustments are most effective if they are just-in-time. Indeed, only small adjustments are required if they are timely and at the right point (see e.g. Land et al. 2015). The planned workload of a station is an effective measure for determining when and where to adjust capacity. This measure is reflected in the load on the salesperson's display.

Chapter 10

Summary: Framework of Applicability

Highlights

- *We discuss the impact of the loop structure, card characteristics and IT requirements on the applicability of card-based systems.*
- *We discuss nested card-based control systems given that most shops have more than one control problem.*
- *We discuss some rather general but important implementation issues.*

Card-based control systems are input/output control systems. This means that they control the input of work in accordance with the output rate. Only if work leaves the shop floor is new work allowed to enter. The information on the output rate is typically provided by cards. This is why they are called card-based systems. While all four card-based control systems discussed in this book—*kanban*, constant work-in-process (ConWIP), paired-cell overlapping loops of cards with authorization (POLCA), and control of balance by card-based navigation (COBACABANA)—are indeed input/output control systems, there are significant differences in terms of how input/output control is realized, i.e. the feedback loop. There are three dimensions to this:

1. The loop structure itself
2. The properties of the information that is circulated in the loop (i.e. the cards)

3. The independence of the loops—i.e. whether additional IT support is required

In this, the concluding chapter, we will contrast our four card-based systems according to these three dimensions and explore the consequences in terms of their applicability to the different control problems.

Loop Structure and Its Implications for the Application of Card-Based Systems

Let's first look at the actual loop structure. The major implications in the light of our criteria for problem diagnosis are summarized in Table 10.1.

Kanban systems and POLCA need to establish a loop for any possible routing step. So both use the same loop structure, and both have to reflect the routing in their loop structure, which limits their applicability to simple routings only. A peculiarity of POLCA is that blocking can occur if the routing is not directed. We saw that this is due to POLCA treating an order control problem as an inventory control problem through the use of job-anonymous cards.

The major difference between *kanban* systems and POLCA is that, for POLCA, a job stays in the loop for two operations, while, for *kanban* systems, jobs only stay in a loop for one operation. So a POLCA loop contains two operations per job, while a *kanban* loop only contains one operation per job. A COBACABANA loop also only contains one operation per job. Meanwhile, a single ConWIP loop contains all of the operations of a job.

ConWIP significantly simplifies the loop structure, but this is only possible if all jobs enter at the same station and leave at the same station. So, its applicability is restricted to the pure flow shop. Moreover, individual stations are not controlled, which arguably prohibits the application of ConWIP to an inventory control problem.

COBACABANA uses a centralized pool and release function that precedes the shop floor. This allows orders to enter the shop floor at any station. Meanwhile, by establishing loops between a central release function and each station—rather than between stations—COBACABANA avoids the need for the loop structure and the routing to overlap. This allows all possible routing permutations to be accommodated.

Table 10.1 Loop Structure and Consequences for the Application of Card-Based Control Systems

	Kanban	ConWIP	POLCA	COBACABANA
Where established?	Between two stations.	Between entry and exit station.	Between two stations.	Between stations and a central release function, which precedes the shop floor.
Relation to routing	Needs to be established for each possible routing step.	One loop must contain all possible routings.	Needs to be established for each possible routing step.	Routing independent.
Contains (operations per order)	One operation.	All operations.	Two operation (for all except the first and last operation, an operation makes part of two loops).	One operation.
WIP-Cap (limit on work in the loop)	Per station.	On shop floor load. Station load is not limited.	Per station.	Per station.
Consequences: inventory/ order separation point	Creates a problem of card propagation in the order control problem since information has to be transmitted via each routing step. This creates direct/ indirect load in each loop and prohibits control in an order control problem.	Does not allow for controlling the work-in-process at each station and should not be applied to an inventory control problem.	Similar structure to *kanban* but problems resolved by card properties. Allows for inventory and order control problems.	Uses a centralized release function to control the mix of orders released to the shop floor. Designed for the order control problem.

Continued

Table 10.1 (Continued) Loop Structure and Consequences for the Application of Card-Based Control Systems

	Kanban	ConWIP	POLCA	COBACABANA
Consequences: routing characteristics	Only allows for simple routings and low routing variability.	Only allows for the pure flow shop, i.e. all work visiting all stations in the same order.	Only allows for simple, directed routings. Leads to blocking if the loop structure is undirected, since jobs waiting in a queue holding a card from a loop typically require a card from another loop to leave the loop.	Allows for all possible routing characteristics.
Consequences: processing time variability	Individual loops keep processing time information local. Does not allow for load balancing across stations.	General loop does not provide processing time information. Does not allow for load balancing across stations.	Individual loops keep processing time information local. Does not allow for load balancing across stations.	Centralized load information provides a global view of the shop floor, which facilitates load balancing across stations.

Card Properties and Their Implications for the Application of Card-Based Systems

Card-based control systems differ widely not only in terms of their loop structure but also in terms of what meaning is conveyed by a card. Ultimately, cards are visual signals. So what do they actually signal? Let's look at the different card properties of card-based systems—with the major implications in the light of our criteria for problem diagnosis summarized in Table 10.2.

There are mainly two differences. First, ConWIP and POLCA cards are (job) anonymous. This means that they just say "a job" has been finished ... (and a new one can start). We saw that, in the case of POLCA, this may lead to blocking. Meanwhile, *kanban* and COBACABANA cards designate the part/job. Second, a particular feature of COBACABANA cards is that their size indicates the processing time requirements of a job. This supports workload balancing considerations on the central planning board.

The Need for IT Support and Its Implications for the Application of Card-Based Systems

The last difference in terms of how feedback loops operate in order to realize input/output control is whether they operate independently or whether they are influenced or supported by IT. The major implications are summarized in Table 10.3.

POLCA relies heavily on IT support. In fact, one of its main features is the need to calculate earliest release dates using material requirements planning (MRP). Also ConWIP systems are typically embedded in IT-based higher-level planning systems. Similarly, *kanban* systems need IT support for realizing *heijunka*; we saw that the *heijunka* box does not provide a tool for supporting workload balancing. In fact, Monden (1983, p. 60) earlier reported that *"Attaining the optimal sequence schedule of mixed production is somewhat difficult, but Toyota is trying to determine such a schedule by applying a heuristic computer program."* Finally, COBACABANA provides a centralized release function that incorporates workload balancing. This allows for detailed decisions concerning which order to release next to the shop floor. It does not require any IT support since, for example, workload balancing calculations can be executed using the simple planning board. This can make COBACABANA particularly attractive to smaller shops with limited financial resources.

Table 10.2 Card Properties and Consequences for the Application of Card-Based Control Systems

	Kanban	ConWIP	POLCA	COBACABANA
What does it say?	A part/product/service was or will be used.	We finished one of the jobs in the system; release another job.	We finished one of the jobs you sent us; you can send us another.	The operation belonging to this part/product at this station has been completed.
Card type(s)	Originally three (in the internal supply chain): withdrawal *kanbans*; work-in-process *kanbans* (was used) and production *kanbans* (will be used); for shop floor control, often reduced to one common *kanban*.	Only one.	Only one.	Two (which appear in pairs): a release card for load balancing calculations and operation card for feedback.
Information conveyed	Which part/product was or will be used and should thus be produced. This may include information on the processing/service time, due date etc.	That the shop floor has capacity to work on another job.	That the next station in the routing of the job has future availability.	Operation card: which job has been completed at which station Operation/release cards: what is the load contribution (processing time) of this operation (given by the size of the cards).

Consequences: Inventory/order separation point	If cards are bound to a specific order (order control problem) they have to wait at a station until all preceding operations have been completed (indirect load). This prohibits their use for order control problems.	A single loop avoids problems as for *kanban*. However, jobs are not prioritized since cards are (job) anonymous. Requires higher-level IT support for creating an appropriate sequence in which jobs are released to the shop floor.	Cards are (job) anonymous, which avoids the problems of *kanbans*. Requires an MRP system for prioritizing jobs according to urgency (earliest release date for each operation).	The centralized release function avoids problems as for *kanban* and ensures prioritizing of jobs.
Consequences: Routing characteristics	None	None	Prohibits feedback loops due to the risk of blocking.	None
Consequences: Processing time variability	Limiting the number of cards does not stabilize the workload if processing times vary since cards and processing times are not associated.	Only gives information on jobs completed by the system. Does not allow for load balancing.	Only gives information on jobs completed at a station. Does not allow for load balancing.	Release cards allow for visualizing the current load situation and job progress on the shop floor. Allows for load balancing. Load balancing calculations are facilitated by the planning board and the release cards.

Table 10.3   Need for IT Support and Consequences for Application of Card-Based Control Systems

	Kanban	*ConWIP*	*POLCA*	*COBACABANA*
Where?	May be required to calculate the production plan for the final station of a process (a *heijunka* box is no calculation device).	Material requirements planning (MRP)-based higher-level planning required for the prioritization of work if not embedded in another system.	Material requirements planning (MRP) system required for the prioritization of work.	No support required.
Consequences	Requires additional investment. Complexity is reintroduced.			Especially suited for small shops (shop floors), which are less likely to have sophisticated IT solutions and infrastructures in place.

Final Considerations: Nested Card-Based Control Systems

Card-based systems are powerful means of controlling production. They are simple and visual; and they have widely "proved their mettle" in practice. However, we have also seen there are important differences in terms of the applicability of each card-based control system. Each has emerged from a specific need as follows:

1. *Kanban* emerged from Toyota's efforts to reduce overproduction waste and other associated wastes, such as inventory and transportation, etc. It is an extremely powerful means of control for the internal supply

chain, i.e. the control of the convergent flows of transformed resources, and for the inventory control problem.

2. ConWIP addressed a major weakness of *kanban* systems, which was that they were designed for an inventory control problem. ConWIP presents a straightforward solution to the order control problem, which had caused major trouble for *kanban* systems. But ConWIP only applies to the pure flow shop—i.e. all orders have to visit all stations in the same order. Moreover, processing time variability has to be low since no load balancing capabilities are incorporated in a ConWIP system.

3. POLCA essentially takes *kanban* cards and makes them (job) anonymous; and it uses an MRP system to prioritize the flow of orders. This provides another solution to the order control problem that accommodates more routing variability than ConWIP. But still, routings need to be simple and directed, and processing time variability has to be low due to a lack of load balancing capabilities.

4. COBACABANA provides a solution for the order control problem. It allows for high-variety routings through the use of an explicit pool that precedes the shop floor. The pool allows for centralized information on the workload of each station. This supports load balancing by selectively releasing a mix of jobs that balances the workload across stations. This makes it applicable to contexts with high variety in processing times. The other systems presented in this book should not be applied in such contexts as they do not have workload balancing capabilities. In fact, COBACABANA is the card-based version of workload control—a production control concept specifically developed for complex job shops. Further, COBACABANA can be easily extended from a focus on order release to also incorporate a means of delivery time estimation to support customer enquiry management.

It follows from these considerations that each card-based system addresses a certain control problem. An overall framework for the applicability of each card-based system is presented in Table 10.4.

While we provide guidance here on choosing between the solutions, as mentioned at the beginning of this book, there are no purity concerns here. A shop often experiences different control problems, which require different solutions. Different card-based systems can in fact be nested or used for different functions to control the shop floor or to link and control different shop floors (remember the level of analysis). An example of a nested system is given in Figure 10.1.

Table 10.4 Card-Based Control Systems: Advantages, Disadvantages, and General Guidelines for Application

	Kanban	*ConWIP*	*POLCA*	*COBACABANA*
Advantages	Simple, effective, visual means for inventory control. Widely applied and tested in practice.	Simple, straightforward.	Extends the use of an inventory control system for order control.	Loop structure allows for all possible routing permutations. Centralized planning board gives overview of the current situation on the shop floor. Supports load balancing.
Disadvantages	Only allows for simple routings and low routing variability. Problems with card-propagation and control in an order control system. Does not provide load balancing.	Only can be applied in the pure flow shop. The work-in-process at a station is not limited. Higher level IT support is needed for the prioritization of work. Does not provide load balancing.	Requires MRP system. The earliest release date calculated by the system may introduce starvation. Only allows for simple, directed routings due to the risk of blocking. Does not provide load balancing.	Requires a change in mind-set compared to the other card-based systems that more or less replicate *kanban*. For example, the routing and card-loop structure are decoupled, cards represent operations (and their processing time by their size), an explicit pool is used, etc.
General guidelines for application	First choice for inventory control problems.	Simple, straightforward solution for an order control problem.	Provides a solution to enhance an existing MRP system.	First choice for complex (high routing and/or processing time variability) order control problems.

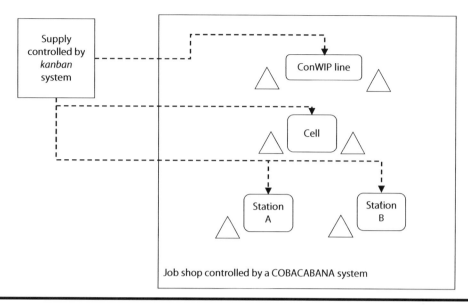

Figure 10.1   Example of a nested *kanban*, COBACABANA, and ConWIP system.

Nested Card-Based Control Systems

According to the level of analysis, different product/service flows can be identified. For example, subassemblies flow together on an assembly shop floor (line, cell, work center, etc.). But each subassembly may have been produced on a different shop floor (line, cell, work center, etc.). Each of these shop floors where the subassemblies are produced may require a different card-based control system. Meanwhile, the coordination of the flow of different subassemblies in the assembly shop may require another card-based control system; so too might the provision of supply. So the shop may consist of different interlinked shop floors (line, cell, work center, etc.), each with a slightly different control problem. This may require an overall card-based control solution that nests various card-based solutions onto each other.

Implementation Information

Let us close out this book with some information on implementation. This, however, is a short section—because we do not believe that a detailed description of prior implementations or approaches facilitates implementation. Each shop has its own idiosyncrasies, culture, etc. As we said at the beginning of this book, card-based systems are not "cookie-cutter" solutions that you buy and things are done. On the contrary, they require dedication, effort, and standing all day on the shop floor, watching, watching, and watching.

This book set out to provide insights into the functioning of card-based systems—primarily to support you in identifying an appropriate solution for your control problem. This knowledge is the key to any successful implementation. Understanding card-based systems is the only required prerequisite for a successful implementation. We just summarize some general implementation guidelines here (see also Figure 10.2).

If you are considering implementing a card-based control system in your company, the first fundamental question you should ask yourself is

- *Is a card-based system the right solution for my shop?*
  By this point in the book, you should have a good idea—and probably wouldn't have got this far if the answer wasn't "yes." Chapter 1 gave

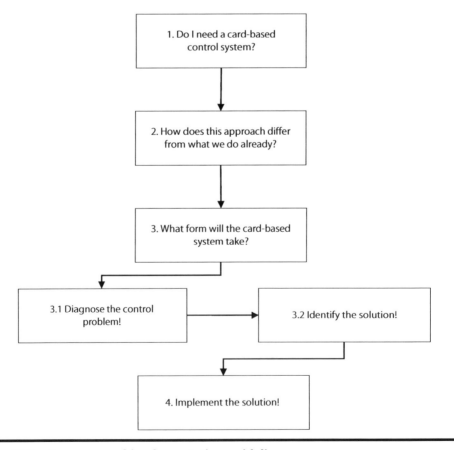

Figure 10.2 Some general implementation guidelines.

some indications on how to answer this question. Having established that a card-based control system is the right solution for you (i.e. that you need it to meet your objectives), it then becomes important to ask the next question.

■ *How does this approach differ from what we do already?*
The greater the degree of change required, the more time and emphasis will be needed in preparing the groundwork for implementation, training personnel, etc. Card-based control systems emphasize, for example, the need to delay the release of orders to stabilize and reduce work-in-process levels. This can be quite a counter-intuitive idea requiring a change in mind-set. Achieving a change in mind-set away, for example, from push to pull (i.e. the later line going to the earlier) was one of the major challenges reported by Taiichi Ohno when implementing *kanban*. You may then ask the next question.

■ *What form will the card-based system take?*
We hope that our book has answered this question. As mentioned several times throughout this book—there are no purity concerns. But start with the problem, not a preconceived idea of what the solution should be. You may nest and combine different systems or even invent your own system (in which case we would like you to contact us).

In terms of the actual physical implementation of the card system, we suggest you consider the following three steps:

1. *Establish the loop structure.* This means that you have to determine a first set of stations (cells, work centers, etc.) that you consider important to control. This may require grouping machines, changing the layout, etc. It should not be fixed but should allow for later adjustments once the system is installed.

2. *Flood it with cards.* This means you should start with a high level of work-in-process in the system. We do not suggest that you start with a tight restriction on the number of cards (or a tight workload norm in the case of COBACABANA) from the outset. Rather, the number of cards (workload norm) should be lowered gradually, always keeping an eye on waste migration—waste migration indicates a buffer and the need for variability reduction. A lot of academic literature has been produced on determining the optimum number of cards in various card-based systems. But this literature is typically based on some very hypothetical system that is unlikely to reflect your reality. So we suggest you start

with a "flooded" system and adjust over time as you learn. For example, this was the original method used for the *kanban* system, as high-lighted by Yasuhiro Monden:

> The actual number of *Kanban*s at each process within Toyota's factories is not determined automatically by the specific formula. ... In fact, each supervisor is given very specific instructions: "You can have as many *Kanban* as you want. You should reduce the number of *Kanban* (i.e. inventory level) one sheet by one sheet down to your minimum possible limit as you are able to improve your process" ... When it is found that the present number of *Kanban* is not suitable and causes trouble in the shop, the number of *Kanban* should be changed (increased) immediately. In a sense, *this is a trial-and-error method*; but this approach is very practical and useful for motivating the supervisor and workers to reduce the number of *Kanban* and improve their process. (Monden 1983, p. 175; our italics)

3. *Keep it flexible.* It is not a case of installing, getting it to run, and that's it. You constantly have to monitor whether the system works as it should or whether it can be improved; or whether the control problem has changed. Over time, the characteristics of the jobs in the shop may change, for example; and this may require changes to be made to the system. Loop structures or even the card-based system itself can always be changed.

We hope that you have enjoyed reading this book and gained the insights required to successfully select, implement, and use card-based systems. All that remains for us is to finish this book with a quote by the King: "A little less conversation, a little more action please" (Elvis Presley).

P.S.: We hope that this book supports you in your quest for simple yet effective production control. If you think we committed significant errors in our presentation of the card-based systems or overlooked important aspects or alternative solutions; or you have an interesting implementation that provides new insights; or you have invented your own system that we should know about; or you just need some more information—please do not hesitate to contact us.

References

Ashby, W. R., 1957, *An Introduction to Cybernetics*, London: Chapman & Hall.

Beer, S., 1994, *Decision and Control: The Meaning of Operational Research and Management Cybernetics*, Chichester, UK: Wiley.

Conway, R., Maxwell, W. L., and Miller, L. W., 1967, *Theory of Scheduling*, Reading, MA: Addison-Wesley.

Ford, H., 1923, *My Life and Work*, Garden City, NY: Doubleday.

Goldratt, E. M. and Cox, J., 2004, *The Goal: A Process of Ongoing Improvement*, 3rd revised edn, Great Barrington, MA: North River Press.

Harada, T., 2015, *Management Lessons from Taiichi Ohno: What Every Leader Can Learn from the Man Who Invented the Toyota Production System*, New York: McGraw-Hill Education.

Hayes, R. H. and Wheelwright, S. C., 1979, "Link manufacturing process and product life cycles," *Harvard Business Review*, (March/April), 127–136.

Hino, S., 2006, *Inside the Mind of Toyota: Management Principles for Enduring Growth*, Cambridge, MA: Productivity Press.

Hopp, W. J. and Spearman, M. L., 2001, *Factory Physics: Foundations of Manufacturing Management*, 2nd edn, New York: McGraw-Hill.

Hopp, W. J. and Spearman, M. L., 2004, "To pull or not to pull: What is the question?" *Manufacturing & Service Operations Management*, 6(2), 133–148.

Kanet, J. J., 1988, "Load-limited order release in job shop scheduling systems," *Journal of Operations Management*, 7(3), 44–58.

Land, M. J., 2009, "COBACABANA (control of balance by card-based navigation): A card-based system for job shop control," *International Journal of Production Economics*, 117, 97–103.

Land, M. J. and Gaalman, G., 1998, "The performance of workload control concepts in job shops: Improving the release method," *International Journal of Production Economics*, 56/57, 347–364.

Land, M. J., Stevenson, M., Thürer, M., and Gaalman, G. J. C., 2015, "Job shop control: In search of the key to delivery improvements," *International Journal of Production Economics*, 168, 257–266.

Little, J., 1961, "A proof of the theorem L = λW," *Operations Research*, 8, 383–387.

Monden, Y., 1983, *Toyota Production System: Practical Approach to Production Management*, Norcross, GA: Industrial Engineering and Management Press.

Ohno, T., 1988, *Toyota Production System: Beyond Large-Scale Production*, 1st edn, Cambridge, MA: Productivity Press.

Oosterman, B., Land, M. L., and Gaalman, G., 2000, "The influence of shop characteristics on workload control," *International Journal of Production Economics*, 68(1), 107–119.

Orlicky, J., 1975, *Material Requirements Planning: The New Way of Life in Production and Inventory Management*, New York: McGraw-Hill.

Plossl, G. W. and Wight, O. W., 1971, "Capacity planning and control," Working Paper presented at the APICS International Conference, St. Louis, MO.

Protzman, C., Mayzell, G., and Kerpchar, J., 2010, *Leveraging Lean in Healthcare: Transforming Your Enterprise into a High Quality Patient Care Delivery System*, 1st edn, Cambridge, MA: Productivity Press.

Riezebos, J., 2010, "Design of POLCA material control systems," *International Journal of Production Research*, 48(5), 1455–1477.

Shingo, S., 1989, *A Study of the Toyota Production System from an Industrial Engineering Viewpoint*, Cambridge, MA: Productivity Press.

Soepenberg, G. D., Land, M. J., and Gaalman, G., 2008, "The order progress diagram: A supportive tool for diagnosing delivery reliability performance in make-to-order companies," *International Journal of Production Economics*, 112(1), 495–503.

Spearman, M. L., Woodruff, D. L., and Hopp, W. J., 1990, "CONWIP: A pull alternative to kanban," *International Journal of Production Research*, 28(5), 879–894.

Sugimori, Y., Kusunoki, K., Cho, F., and Uchikawa, S., 1977, "Toyota production system and Kanban system materialization of just-in-time and respect-for-human system," *International Journal of Production Research*, 15(6), 553–564.

Suri, R., 1989, *Quick Response Manufacturing: A Companywide Approach to Reducing Leadtimes*, Cambridge, MA: Productivity Press.

Suri, R., 2010, *It's About Time: The Competitive Advantage of Quick Response Manufacturing*, Cambridge, MA: Productivity Press.

Thompson, J. D., 1967, *Organizations in Action: Social Science Bases for Administrative Theory*, 1st edn, New York: McGraw-Hill.

Thürer, M., Land, M. J., and Stevenson, M., 2014b, "Card-based workload control for job shops: Improving COBACABANA," *International Journal of Production Economics*, 147, 180–188.

Thürer, M., Stevenson, M., and Protzman, C. W., 2015, "COBACABANA (control of balance by card based navigation): An alternative to kanban in the pure flow shop?" *International Journal of Production Economics*, 166, 143–151.

Thürer, M., Stevenson, M., Silva, C., Land, M. J., and Fredendall, L. D., 2012, "Workload control (WLC) and order release: A Lean solution for make-to-order companies," *Production & Operations Management*, 21(5), 939–953.

Thürer, M., Stevenson, M., Silva, C., Land, M. J., Fredendall, L. D., and Melnyk, S. A., 2014a, "Lean control for make-to-order companies: Integrating customer enquiry management and order release," *Production & Operations Management*, 23(3), 463–476.

Weber, M., 2014, *Wirtschaft und Gesellschaft: Soziologie*, Studienausgabe der MaxWeber Gesamtausgabe Band I/23, Mohr Siebeck, Tubingen.

Wiendahl, H.-P., 1995, *Load-Oriented Manufacturing Control*, Berlin: Springer.

Wight, O., 1970, "Input/output control a real handle on lead time," *Production and Inventory Management Journal*, 11(3), 9–31.

Appendix: Summary of Card-Based Systems

This Appendix provides a quick overview of each of the card-based systems that we have discussed in this book. This includes information on further reading in case you wish to know more.

Kanban Systems

Kanban *systems are powerful solutions to inventory control problems with low routing and processing time variability.*

Kanban systems were originally developed for the internal supply chain, i.e. to link the flow of different products/services—similar to a river and its confluences. Starting from the main line, the later line signals to the earlier line what "was" (in the case of a work-in-process *kanban* system) or "will be" (in the case of a production *kanban* system) needed. A withdrawal *kanban* is used to withdraw the product (e.g. part) from the earlier (or secondary) line. In a work-in-process *kanban* system, once a part is withdrawn, a work-in-process *kanban* is freed and signals to the beginning of the secondary (or earlier) line to replenish the withdrawn product. In a production *kanban* system, the production *kanban* signals the future use, and the product is produced so as to arrive at the withdrawing station when it is needed. The structure of a work-in-process *kanban* system is illustrated in Figure A.1, while the structure of a production *kanban* system is illustrated in Figure A.2.

The system changes when we move from an internal supply chain to a shop floor control problem, i.e. the coordination of independent product/service flows through the same transforming resources. Two cards are

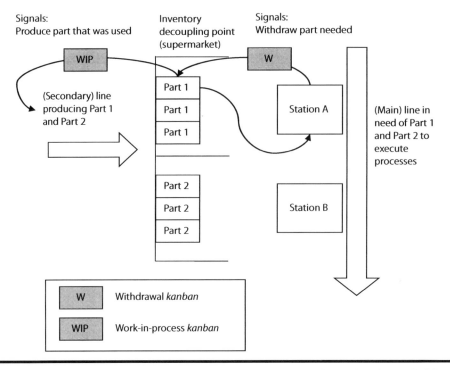

Figure A.1 Work-in-process *kanban* system for the internal supply chain (linking product/service flows).

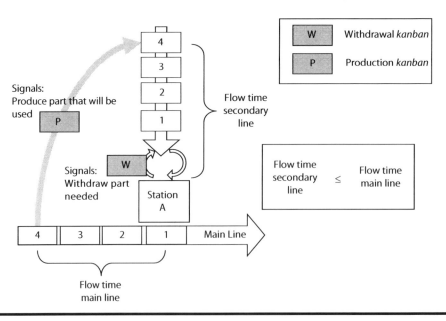

Figure A.2 Production *kanban* system for the internal supply chain (linking product/ service flows).

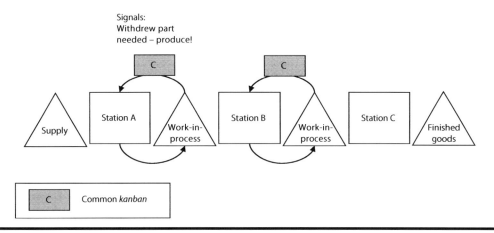

Figure A.3   Common *kanban* system for shop floor control.

typically not required anymore—since work directly flows into the queue of the next station, feedback loops can be combined. The resulting single *kanban* is called a common *kanban*. It is illustrated in Figure A.3.

For *kanban* systems, a *kanban* loop needs to be established for each routing step. This restricts the applicability of *kanban* systems to shops with simple routing characteristics (i.e. low routing variability). Moreover, if the flow of orders is controlled (i.e. in the order control problem, where each transformed resource has a genidentity), cards need to propagate information backward for each routing step. They then have to wait for the order to arrive. During this wait, a *kanban* card represents indirect load; therefore, more than one card should be allowed in each *kanban* loop to allow for the work at the station (direct load) and the work that is still at an upstream station (the indirect load). This results in the last station in the routing requiring the highest number of *kanbans* and jeopardizes effective control. *Kanban* systems should consequently not be applied to an order control problem.

In general, *kanban* systems do not allow for workload balancing. Therefore, they should not be applied in environments with high processing time variability, since these environments require some form of load balancing to avoid unnecessary (or premature) starvation at downstream stations.

Further Reading

Monden, Y., 1983, *Toyota Production System: Practical Approach to Production Management*, Norcross, GA: Industrial Engineering and Management Press.

Ohno, T., 1988, *Toyota Production System: Beyond Large-Scale Production*, 1st edn, Cambridge, MA: Productivity Press.

Shingo, S., 1989, *A Study of the Toyota Production System from an Industrial Engineering Viewpoint*, Cambridge, MA: Productivity Press.

Sugimori, Y., Kusunoki, K., Cho, F., and Uchikawa, S., 1977, "Toyota production system and Kanban system materialization of just-in-time and respect-for-human system," *International Journal of Production Research*, 15(6), 553–564.

The ConWIP System

ConWIP is a simple and powerful solution to the order control problem in a pure flow shop with low processing time variability.

Constant work-in-process (ConWIP) avoids propagation from station to station by linking the last station of the line with the first station of the line. This means it ignores the difference between direct and indirect load altogether. Whenever a job leaves the line, a new job can be released; hence, the number of jobs in the line is regulated. A ConWIP system is illustrated in Figure A.4.

An important feature that distinguishes ConWIP from a production or work-in-process *kanban*, as used in the internal supply chain, is that ConWIP cards are anonymous. Thus, they signal that "some job" is completed and another "job" can start, not that a "specific job" was or will be used. This shifts the decision concerning which job to start on the line next to the first station in the process.

ConWIP should not be applied to inventory control problems since it does not control the work at each station. ConWIP also requires the same first and last station to be present in the routing of all products/services that flow through the shop floor. Since lines should also not split, the applicability of ConWIP is essentially restricted to pure flow shops, i.e. where each

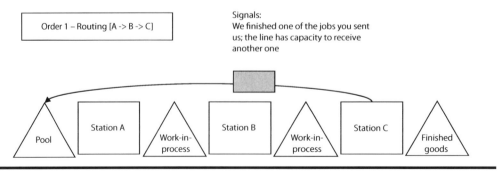

Figure A.4 ConWIP system (i.e. anonymous cards).

order visits each station in the same sequence. Another important shortcoming is that lines should not be too long, since the minimum number of jobs in the system must be equal to the number of stations in the loop to allow for at least one job at each station. Since the number of jobs at each station is not controlled, all jobs could also queue at just one station, which would result in extreme overload.

ConWIP does not support load balancing and should consequently only be applied in environments with low processing time variability. This is the most critical issue since ConWIP is applied to pure flow shops—and starvation caused by processing time variability is particularly evident in pure flow shops, since the input of work to a station is directly dependent on the processing times at upstream stations.

Further Reading

Hopp, W. J. and Spearman, M. L., 2001, *Factory Physics: Foundations of Manufacturing Management*, 2nd edn, New York: McGraw-Hill.

Spearman, M. L., Hopp, W. J., and Woodruff, D. L., 1989, "An hierarchical control architecture for Constant Work-in-Process (CONWIP) Production Systems," *Journal of Manufacturing and Operations Management*, 2, 147–171.

Spearman, M. L., Woodruff, D. L., and Hopp, W. J., 1990, "CONWIP: A pull alternative to kanban," *International Journal of Production Research*, 28(5), 879–894.

The POLCA System

POLCA is a solution to the order control problem so long as routing variability is low, routing is directed, and processing time variability is low. It is particularly suitable if a material requirements planning (MRP) system is already used for material control.

Paired-cell overlapping loops of cards with authorization (POLCA) combines a *kanban*-like card system (but with (job) anonymous cards) and an MRP system. The MRP system is required because, like ConWIP cards, POLCA cards do not convey which order to work on—only that something can be worked on. So some other means of prioritization is required. Ignoring the genidentity of orders, however, transforms the order control problem into an inventory control problem. So POLCA is essentially a card-based inventory control solution used for an order control problem with the help of an MRP system. The MRP system calculates an earliest release date

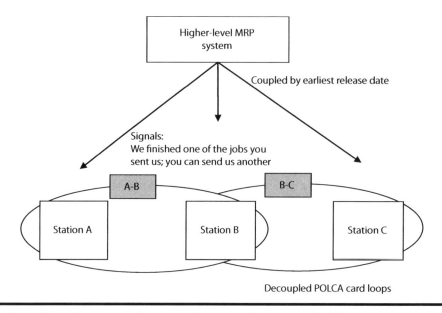

Figure A.5   POLCA system (decoupled POLCA loops coupled by an MRP system).

for each operation, which needs to be reached before an operation can take place. This interplay between MRP and the card-based system is illustrated in Figure A.5.

POLCA loops are quite complex. When an order that must travel through the A-B loop arrives at Station A, four things are needed to start an operation in POLCA:

■ The transformed resource needs to have arrived at Station A.
■ Station A must be available.
■ The earliest release date for the transformed resource at Station A must have been reached.
■ The POLCA A-B card, and thus future availability (capacity) of Station B, must be available.

Once the operation is complete at Station A, the job moves to Station B where it has to wait for another POLCA card (from the next station in its routing, e.g. Station C). Once the order is completed at Station B, and only then, the POLCA card is sent back to Station A, which authorizes further work to start at Station A. This closes the A-B loop.

Treating the order control problem as an inventory control problem makes POLCA more suitable for the former when compared to *kanban* systems. However, it may lead to severe blocking if the routing is not directed.

Moreover, the fact that the earliest release date needs to have been reached for an operation to start introduces most of the weaknesses of a push system. In fact, if earliest release dates are too late, severe starvation is introduced since, even if stations A and B are starving, the operation can only begin once the earliest release date has been reached. If earliest release dates are too early, prioritization cannot be ensured.

As for *kanban*, POLCA's loop structure needs to cover each routing step. So POLCA suffers from the same restrictions as a *kanban* system—only simple, direct routings can be accommodated.

Finally, POLCA does not support load balancing and should consequently only be applied in environments with low processing time variability to avoid starvation caused by processing time variability.

Further Reading

Krishnamurthy, A. and Suri, R., "Planning and implementing POLCA: A card-based control system for high variety or custom engineered products," *Production Planning and Control*, 20(7), 596–610.

Riezebos, J., 2010, "Design of POLCA material control systems," *International Journal of Production Research*, 48(5), 1455–1477.

Suri, R., 1989, *Quick Response Manufacturing: A Companywide Approach to Reducing Leadtimes*, Cambridge, MA: Productivity Press.

Suri, R., 2010, *It's About Time: The Competitive Advantage of Quick Response Manufacturing*, Cambridge, MA: Productivity Press.

The COBACABANA System

Control of balance by card-based navigation (COBACABANA) provides a powerful solution to the order control problem for complex high-variety shops with high routing and/or processing time variability.

COBACABANA uses a central release function that precedes the shop floor. Orders do not immediately enter the shop floor but are retained in a so-called pre-shop pool from where they are released to meet performance targets, such as achieving a low, stable work-in-process level at each station and high on-time delivery to the customer. Meanwhile, the centralized release function is supported by card loops between each station and the release function. Card loops provide information on which operation has been completed. So COBACABANA cards are bound to a specific operation (and thus to the corresponding station and job). To support load balancing calculations on the planning board, cards are (i) duplicated, so one card (the release card) can stay on the planning board, visualizing the workload on the shop floor while the other (the operation card) provides feedback from the shop floor; and (ii) represent the workload of each operation by their size.

Orders are only released to the shop floor if their workload contribution to each station in their routing fits a pre-established workload norm. So the workload released to each station, as visualized by the release cards on the planning board, is limited. This workload to each station may either be measured in aggregate load (shops with directed routings) or corrected aggregate load units (shops with undirected routings). Keeping the workload within norms creates a mix of orders on the shop floor that balances the workload across stations. The overall structure of COBACABANA's shop floor control mechanism is illustrated in Figure A.6.

The introduction of the pre-shop pool allows orders to enter the shop floor at any station. Meanwhile, the loop structure between a station and the centralized release function accommodates all possible routing steps. So, COBACABANA allows for accommodating all possible routing permutations.

COBACABANA also provides a unique load balancing capability, since this function is integrated into the release decision. This allows for accommodating high processing time variability.

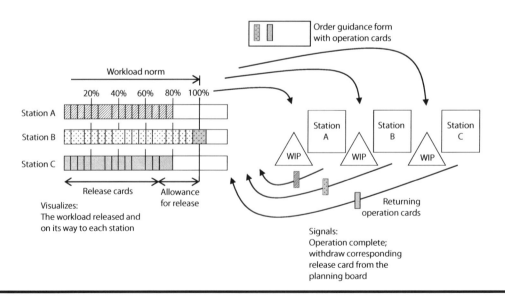

Figure A.6 COBACABANA release—using loops between a central release function and each station on the shop floor.

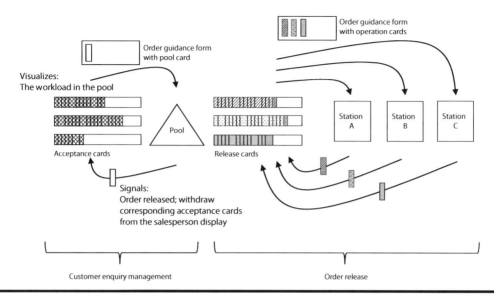

Figure A.7   COBACABANA—integrating delivery date estimation and order release control.

In addition, COBACABANA provides a simple extension that allows for estimating delivery times. The calculation of delivery time estimates is supported by the salesperson's display, which visualizes the load in the pool waiting to be released to a station. A pool waiting time can be estimated using Little's Law and the release rate of a station. Since operation throughput times are stabilized by order release, the delivery time allowance can then be estimated by the pool waiting time plus a constant allowance for the operation throughput times on the shop floor plus an external allowance to account for variability between the estimated and realized delivery time.

Overall, COBACBANA provides a comprehensive card-based control solution, as illustrated in Figure A.7.

Further Reading

Land, M. J., 2009, "COBACABANA (control of balance by card-based navigation): A card-based system for job shop control," *International Journal of Production Economics*, 117, 97–103.

Thürer, M., Land, M. J., and Stevenson, M., 2014b, "Card-based workload control for job shops: Improving COBACABANA," *International Journal of Production Economics*, 147, 180–188.

Thürer, M., Land, M. J., Stevenson, M., Fredendall, L. D., and Godinho, F. M., 2015a, "Concerning workload control and order release: The pre-shop pool sequencing decision," *Production & Operations Management*, 24(7), 1179–1192.

Thürer, M., Stevenson, M., and Protzman, C. W., 2015b, "COBACABANA (control of balance by card based navigation): An alternative to kanban in the pure flow shop?" *International Journal of Production Economics*, 166, 143–151.

Thürer, M., Stevenson, M., Silva, C., Land, M. J., and Fredendall, L. D., 2012, "Workload control (WLC) and order release: A Lean solution for make-to-order companies," *Production & Operations Management*, 21(5), 939–953.

Thürer, M., Stevenson, M., Silva, C., Land, M. J., Fredendall, L. D., and Melnyk, S. A., 2014a, "Lean control for make-to-order companies: Integrating customer enquiry management and order release," *Production & Operations Management*, 23(3), 463–476.

Index